THE PROGRAMME MANAGERS COMPANION

David E Marsh

London: The Stationery Office

British Library Cataloguing in Publication Data
Marsh, David
Programme Managers Companion -
ISBN 0 11 702840 1
First published in 2001 by:
The Stationery Office Norwich
Editorial Office: The Stationery Office

Published by The Stationery Office Limited and available from:

The Stationery Office
(mail, telephone and fax orders only)
PO Box 29, Norwich NR3 1GN
Telephone orders/enquiries 0870 600 5522
Fax orders 0870 600 5533

Internet http://www.clicktso.com

The Stationery Office Bookshops
123 Kingsway, London WC2B 6PQ
020 7242 6393 Fax 020 7242 6394
68–69 Bull Street, Birmingham B4 6AD
0121 236 9696 Fax 0121 236 9699
33 Wine Street, Bristol BS1 2BQ
0117 926 4306 Fax 0117 924 4515
9–21 Princess Street, Manchester M60 8AS
0161 834 7201 Fax 0161 833 0634
16 Arthur Street, Belfast BT1 4GD
028 9023 8451 Fax 028 9023 5401
The Stationery Office Oriel Bookshop
18–19 High Street, Cardiff CF1 2BZ
029 2039 5548 Fax 029 2038 4347
71 Lothian Road, Edinburgh EH3 9AZ
0870 606 5566 Fax 0870 606 5588

The Stationery Office's Accredited Agents
(see Yellow Pages)

and through good booksellers

Printed in the UK by The Stationery Office Limited, London
TJ5073 C3 09/01

Programme Management Lifecycle

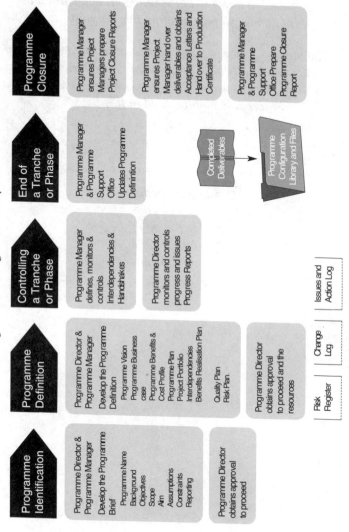

Programme Identification

Programme Director & Programme Manager
Develop the Programme Brief

Programme Name
Background
Objectives
Scope
Aim
Assumptions
Constraints
Reporting

Programme Director obtains approval to proceed

Programme Definition

Programme Director & Programme Manager
Develop the Programme Definition

Programme Vision
Programme Business case
Programme Benefits & Cost Profile
Programme Plan
Project Portfolio
Interdependences
Benefits Realisation Plan

Quality Plan
Risk Plan

Programme Director obtains approval to proceed and the resources

Controlling a Tranche or Phase

Programme Manager defines, monitors & controls
Interdependencies & Handshakes

Programme Director monitors and controls progress and issues
Progress Reports

End of a Tranche or Phase

Programme Manager & Programme Support Office
Updates Programme Definition

Completed Deliverables → Programme Configuration Library and Files

Programme Closure

Programme Manager ensures Project Managers prepare Project Closure Reports

Programme Manager ensures Project Manager hand over deliverables and obtains Acceptance Letters and Hand over to Production Certificate

Programme Manager & Programme Support Office Prepare Programme Closure Report

Risk Register | Change Log | Issues and Action Log

Programme Managers Companion

This book is based on the consultancy advice MMP have provided to assist with the practical application of Programme Management in many organisations.

The author wishes in particular to acknowledge the Post Office who kindly allowed some of the material that was developed for the use of Programme Management in their organisation be used in this book.

This book is dedicated to
Alan Twine
and the team of the
Post Office Counters
Programme Consultancy Unit

Programme Managers Companion

CONTENTS

SECTION ONE: INTRODUCTION TO THE
Programme Managers Companion

1.1 The Purpose of the *Programme Managers Companion*

This book is designed for Programme Managers and provides an overview of programme management and how it is applied. It has been developed to provide day to day assistance and guidance on the activities needed in the management and control of programmes. The *Programme Managers Companion* is not meant to be used in isolation and is designed to support the training given in Programme Management.

It is not designed to be read as a book – rather to be used as a reference manual. Therefore the Programme Manager should use the individual sections as required.

The *Programme Managers Companion* is designed for the average or normal type of programme therefore, it will need to be applied pragmatically and tailored to the needs of a specific programme. The *Programme Managers Companion* is designed to cover all the processes involved in a programme from the identification that a programme is needed, through to its eventual closure.

The processes and outputs contained in the *Programme Managers Companion* are consistent with the OGC's guidance on programme management "Managing Successful Programmes" published in 1999.

The techniques and outputs described in this handbook are based on those developed and used in a number of organisations.

1.2 How to Use The *Programme Managers Companion*

The *Programme Managers Companion* is divided into 4 sections which correspond with the four major processes that the Programme Manager has to perform or oversee.

Each section contains an explanation of the individual process that needs to be performed and also guidance notes on the major activities to be undertaken. At the end of each section is a brief checklist, which explains:

– What processes are to be completed, and who is involved in them.
– The documents or outputs that should be produced.

1.3 The Structure of this Companion

The main body of the *Programme Managers Companion* (sections 2-7) gives an overview of the processes and outputs that need to be developed during the programme. Detailed guidance on the techniques described in the main body of the *Programme Managers Companion* and examples of the outputs that will be produced are given in the Supporting Techniques section. A Glossary of terms is also provided.

SECTION TWO: WHAT IS PROGRAMME MANAGEMENT AND WHY IS IT REQUIRED?

2.1 What is Programme Management?

There are a number of definitions of the term Programme Management – the OGC one being

"Programme Management is the co-ordinated management of a portfolio of projects that change organisations to achieve benefits that are of strategic importance."

Managing Successful Programmes 1999

The purpose of programme management is to effectively integrate and co-ordinate programmes of work which are designed to provide major sustainable benefits for the organisation. It is designed to provide a management framework, or a way of thinking, which is supported by processes that enables an organisation to manage the implementation of changes in a way that allows it to respond to a changing business environment and evolving business strategy.

Indeed it even deals with the need to change this vision of the outcome of the programme as it is subjected to a changing business environment and/or constantly evolving business strategy.

Using programme management is vital if an organisation is to maintain a strategic view and control over a set of projects, work packages or initiatives and their interdependencies, to ensure that these are aligned to support or deliver particular business strategies.

Thus programmes either initiate, adopt or allocate, projects, work packages or initiatives that are needed to:

- create new products;
- create new services;
- effect changes in business operations;
- achieve the vision envisaged in a strategy;
- deliver defined business benefits.

Successful use of programme management depends on knowing and understanding why it is needed and to ensure that it is used effectively and in line with the organisation's culture and existing business processes.

The adoption of the use of programme management will require new interfaces to existing management processes in an organisation – particularly the way the organisation commissions or controls projects, work packages and initiatives. In addition it will also affect the organisations budgeting, financial accounting and resource management processes.

The advice provided in the *Programme Managers Companion* has been derived from many organisations that have successfully adopted programme management. However like all "methods" it will need to be adjusted to reflect the specific needs of each programme.

2.2 Why do Organisations need Programme Management?

When undertaking a large programme of work it is important that it is managed as a whole not just as individual projects, work packages and/or initiatives. The programme's objectives should drive the constituent projects, work packages and or initiatives – not the other way round.

Without programme management, experience in a number of organisations has shown that up to 30% of the current effort being expended is being wasted because:

- duplications of effort – two or more activities doing the same thing;
- activities being performed when the deliverables are no longer required or different deliverables are required;
- activities being performed which do not support the current business strategy or policy;
- common or related activities are not grouped together to obtain economies of scale in terms of the ratio of effort to deliverables, or effective use of skills and expenditure.

In addition to ensuring that these dis-benefits are tackled the use of programme management also provides benefits.

These were summarised in the OGC's guidance on programme management as:

Delivery of Change
More effective delivery of changes because they are planned and implemented in an integrated way, taking care not to affect current business operations adversely.

Cohesion or Alignment Between Strategy and Project Levels
Effective response to disparate initiatives from the top, filling the gap between strategies and projects.

Management Support
Support to senior management who need to keep activities focused on business change objectives.

Resource Management
Improved resource management, project prioritisation and project integration.

Risk Management
Better management of risk because the wider context is understood and explicitly acknowledged.

Benefits Realisation
Help to achieve real business benefits through a formal process of their measurement, management, realisation and sustainability.

Management Control
Improved control through a framework where introducing new infrastructure, standards and quality regimes can be, measured and assessed.

Business Operations
Clarifying how new business operations will deliver improved performance.

Management of Business Case
Building and maintaining a Business Case that clearly compares current business operations with the more beneficial future business operations.

Co-ordination and Control
Co-ordinating and controlling the often complex range of activities necessary to bring about change and improvement.

Transition Management
Defining and driving through the transition from current to future business operations.

Consistency
Introducing and enforcing a consistent system of new or amended policies, standards and work practices.

2.3 How Programme Management differs from Project Management

Programme management concentrates on the achievement of business benefits, whilst project management is about the delivery of a specific component, procedure or system. Programme management defines and commissions this portfolio of projects, work packages or initiatives and monitors how well they are achieving the required business benefits. If necessary programme management will modify or change the contents of the programme to ensure that the required benefits are delivered.

2.4 The differences between Programmes and Projects

The main difference between a programme and a project, is that a project is aimed at the delivery of a defined, agreed specific output or deliverable which do not materially change during the implementation of the project.

A programme however is directed and managed to achieve a vision or business benefits. The outputs or path used to facilitate the delivery of the vision or benefits are adjusted during the implementation of the programme to reflect changes in the business environment and, the success or failure of the component parts of that programme.

Another major difference is that benefits in a project are usually realised after it has been completed – whilst in a programme it is likely that benefits will be realised during its development.

And finally, another major difference is that in a programme it is very likely that a specific project, work package and or initiative will not in itself deliver any benefits, but will enable others to provide benefits.

Programme Managers Companion

OGC's guidance on programme management compared the two approaches and described these differences in the form of a table:

Projects	Programmes
An intense and focused activity that is driven by the outputs that are delivered.	Broad spread activity more concerned with defined change objectives.
The change control mechanisms are present but they are designed to minimise the amount of change undertaken during the project.	The change control mechanisms are designed to support the dynamic definition and management of the outputs required from the project, work packages and or initiatives. Controlled change is expected and welcomed.
Is suited to the management of a specific product, service or outcome.	Produces, through synergy a wider set of benefits than the total of the individual project benefits.
Accrues benefits at the end, or after the project has been completed.	Is aimed at delivering benefits both during and after the conclusion of the programme.
Projects continue until they deliver what has been agreed or defined in the Business Case.	The programme continues until the organisation has achieved the Blueprint – which may be long after the last of the projects has been completed. Similarly the programme may be closed early (before the projects are completed) if the Blueprint has been achieved.

As a consequence of these differences it is all too easy for tensions to arise between programmes and projects in respect of the need of projects to complete on time and to budget and, the need of the wider goals and targets of the programme. It is vital therefore that when projects are contained within programmes that the project management team understand and works with the programme management concepts and structures.

2.5 The Types of Programmes

There are many ways to describe the types of programmes that can be found. The first of these is the scenario or the background to the programme.

For example:

Single Vision Programmes
Where projects, work packages and/or initiatives are selected or adopted to become part of achieving the vision, or are all related or directed towards a common goal.

Unconnected Projects
The management of an unconnected portfolio of projects, work packages and/or initiatives.

Multi Organisation Partnerships
Where each part provides an input to a shared vision – where each part has its own objectives which it hopes to achieve alongside those of the shared vision.

Another way of categorising programmes is in terms of what they are designed to address. For example:

Strategic Programmes
Where the project, work packages and or initiatives are aimed at moving the business towards achieving a set of predefined objectives, targets or goals.

Business Cycle Programmes
Where the multiple projects work packages and initiatives are co-ordinated within a cyclic financial or resource constraint e.g. where they are funded from a single budget allocation.

A Very Large Complex Single Objective Project
Where a project is so large that it is divided into subprojects but must be managed as a whole – e.g. large construction projects.

Infrastructure Programme

Where the programme consists of unrelated projects that together provide an infrastructure of standards or other elements that assist the organisation that move forward the organisation's goals.

Research and or Development Programmes

Where many independent projects, work packages, and/or initiatives are assessed and refocused with certain defined interim and long-term goals.

Partnership Programmes

Where organisations enter into innovative partnership arrangements to sponsor and manage a programme.

What is important however is not that a programme needs to be classified into a type or group – rather that the programme management framework is applied to the programme.

SECTION THREE: PROGRAMME MANAGEMENT ROLES AND RESPONSIBILITIES

3.1 Why is a Programme Organisation Structure needed?

Organisations commission programmes to achieve business benefits. This simple fact is very often lost sight of during the "cut and thrust" of the execution of the development activities. The organisation structure is there to ensure that:

- the organisation retains control;
- the organisation understands its responsibilities for the programme or project;
- the Programme Manager receives any required direction from the "right" person;
- the rest of the organisation knows whom to contact about the programme or project;
- the Programme Manager knows whom to contact about what;
- management of the programme is effected efficiently.

In addition the use of these defined structures and accompanying role descriptions enables the organisation to build into future programmes lessons learnt about the effectiveness or otherwise of the structure.

The theory underpinning all such organisation structures is that the management of a programme needs to deal with the three main issues of:

- why we need to invest in the programme;
- what the programme is to deliver or achieve;
- how the programme is delivered.

The first two are clearly the responsibility of senior management in the organisation and the other the Programme Manager. Without a formal structure with defined roles and responsibilities, it is quite often found that responsibility "flip over" occurs, the senior managers become pre-occupied with <u>How</u> the programme is delivered whilst the <u>What</u> and <u>Why</u> are dealt with by the programme team.

The other major problem that the use of this structure seeks to address is that of the rule of nine. This rule refers to situations that unless you have a structure with defined responsibilities, the Programme Manager will typically have nine meetings with management to get a decision.

The overall organisation structure used to manage programmes and constituent projects is illustrated in the next section, with each of the roles and responsibilities explained, at high level.

The application or deployment of programme management should not automatically mean that the organisation needs to take on additional resources because in most instances they are logical roles that for most organisations will be simple extensions of their existing responsibilities.

However, in the case of very large programmes there may well be justification to employ specialist staff for the role of Programme Manager and programme support.

What is important is that the impact of these additional roles and responsibilities on a person's normal workload is realistically assessed and adjusted to take account of these new responsibilities.

One important consideration is the culture of the organisation – however competent the staff and the efficiency and effectiveness of the processes used, it is vital that the culture of the organisation changes to support the concepts of programme management. The effective use of programme management requires an informed and flexible management regime where issues and risks are openly discussed and evaluated. This will require the organisation to perhaps create such an environment or culture at the same time as implementing programme management. This can cause stresses to emerge between programme management and business as usual processes and beliefs.

To help create this culture it is vital that the senior management is briefed and understands the changes that adopting programme management will require and put in place the necessary changes to the culture.

The following section describes the typical organisation structure used to support programme management. Each organisation must tailor this to reflect the specific needs and culture of the organisation – what is important is that all these responsibilities are addressed in the structure that is implemented.

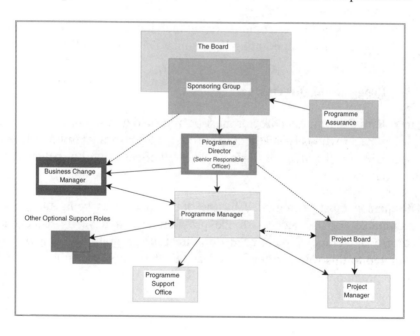

Programme Managers Companion

13

3.2   The Sponsoring Group

All programmes require sponsorship from the most senior – Executive level managers in the organisation or the group of organisations involved in the programme. When more than one organisation is sponsoring the programme, it is essential that the relative contribution from each organisation is established and understood by all the organisations involved in the programme. In such cases it likely that in addition to the individual boards undertaking the sponsorship of the programme, there may be a joint sponsorship group established (at a similar level) consisting of representatives of the boards or sponsors from each of the organisations involved (Sponsoring Group). The specific role and responsibilities of the sponsors are to:

- provide strategic direction and agrees the Blueprint (quantified *Vision* statement);
- be responsible for commissioning individual programmes – setting objectives and appointing Programme Directors and Programme Managers.

3.3   Programme Director

The role of Programme Director must be allocated to a senior or executive level manager who is typically drawn from the Sponsoring Group or Board responsible for the areas of business that will effect or will be affected by the programme.

This person must be regarded by the organisation/s as being ultimately accountable for the success of the programme and have the necessary authority and empowerment needed to direct the programme. This person appointed to this role is often known as the "Senior Responsible Officer" for the programme.

In some programmes where there are a number of such managers it may well be necessary to form a Programme Board to provide a wide enough span of control.

The person allocated the role of Programme Director must have strong leadership and decision making skills. The most successful Programme Directors are able to combine realism with openness – they also have to be able to analyse situations and effectively communicate the Blueprint for the programme. Particular skills that are needed are:

- strategic decision making;
- leadership;
- ability to assess and understand the business information relevant to the programme;
- face validity – a stature that is respected by the sponsors and other managers involved in the programme;
- presentation and communication skills;

The specific responsibilities of this role are:

- ownership of the programme and its vision;
- overall control of the programme and its implementation;
- accountable for achieving the planned success and benefits;
- setting the direction of the individual programme and ensure it is in line with the current and evolving business needs of the organisation;
- overall control of the programme and specific responsibility for the programme's achievements;
- establishing the programme, ensuring it has sufficient resources monitoring progress and the realisation and sustainability of the benefits;

- securing the investment required to execute the programme and realise and sustain the benefits;
- managing the expectations of the programmes stakeholders (the stakeholders are defined in the Blueprint);
- ensuring that the programme effectively manages the changes to the organisation and the attitude of the staff who are affected by the programme;
- managing external and internal communications about the programme;
- commissioning reviews to assess the achievement of the projects and the realisation of the benefits.

3.4   Programme Manager

The Programme Manager is responsible for the delivery of the new capability through the management of the portfolio of projects, work packages and or initiatives on behalf of the Programme Director and the Sponsoring Group.

The specific responsibilities typically include:

- the management of the definition, delivery and sustainability of the programmes benefits;
- the management of the programmes portfolio of projects;
- managing the programmes budget on behalf of the Programme Director;
- planning the programme, monitoring the progress made with the delivery of the programme, resolving issues and instigating control action as required;
- monitoring and reporting on the progress made and the expenditure and resources consumed;
- facilitating the appointment of the members of the project management teams;

- ensuring the programme makes efficient use of resources it has been allocated;
- ensuring the outputs from the programme and its projects conform to the agreed quality standards;
- managing third party contributions to the programme;
- management of the interdependencies and "handshakes" between
- the projects and their component parts;
- identification, assessment and management of risks to the programme;
- identifying any gaps in the ability of the programme to deliver the required benefits and initiating remedial action.

Therefore, the person selected for this role must have strong leadership and management skills. Experience as a Project Manager may be useful but is not compulsory. The most important attribute is that of being able to develop and maintain effective working relationships with the executive and senior managers and the members of the project management teams whether internal or external to the organisation.

Some of the specific skills that the Programme Manager must have are:

- excellent interpersonal and communication skills;
- sufficient seniority and credibility to advise all members of the organisation about the programme and the portfolio of activities that are being undertaken to deliver the programme;
- excellent at problem analysis and developing innovative solutions;
- a full understanding of the organisations budgeting and resource/allocation processes;
- the ability to create the sense of a programme community amongst the members of the projects, work packages and or initiatives delivery teams;
- a good understanding of the techniques used in planning, monitoring and controlling programmes;

Programme Managers Companion

- excellent at written and oral presentations;
- a good understanding of the project management methods used by the organisation.

The Programme Manager has to concentrate activities on the management of the programme "not doing it". In particular ensuring that they do not become super Project Managers. One important way of adopting this management approach is the focus that the Programme Manager takes to the development and monitoring of the Programme Plan.

The Programme Plan is not just a summary of the individual projects, work packages and/or initiatives – it is an extract from those plans which identifies those points in the programme where programme milestones will be achieved and, where major "handshakes" and interdependencies occur between the constituent parts of the portfolio. It is vital that the Programme Plan shows how the objectives of the programme will be delivered.

In monitoring the progress made with the delivery of the programme it is vital to focus on these "handshakes" and interdependencies, rather than the milestones in the constituent projects, work packages and or initiatives.

Thus the typical day to day duties of the Programme Manager are:

- the day to day management of the programme and its budget and the co-ordination of the constituent projects;
- monitoring and reporting on the expenditure and costs and progress achieved as compared to the plan;
- ensuring the portfolio of projects, work packages and/or initiatives will provide the required benefits profile;
- ensuring the contribution that the projects, work packages and/or initiatives make to the attainment of the Blueprint is defined and agreed and that the portfolio contains all the activities needed to deliver the Blueprint;

- ensure that the Programme Plan will provide benefits as defined in the Benefit Profile and follows the priorities established through the assessment of the contribution that the projects, work packages and/or initiatives make to the Blueprint;
- developing and overseeing the implementation of the Benefits Realisation and Sustainability Plan;
- defining the key programme milestones, "handshakes" and interdependencies, the programmes review points and Tranches;
- ensuring that the programme level outputs – e.g. new products or services are to the appropriate level of quality;
- ensuring the programmes resources are deployed and used efficiently and effectively;
- management of inter/intra programme dependencies;
- managing third party contributions to the programme;
- communications with stakeholders;
- assessment and development of a Risk Management Plan and ensuring relevant action has been taken.

3.5   Business Change Manager

The Business Change Manager is the senior level manager who ensures on behalf of the Sponsoring Group that the planned benefits or outcomes are achieved.

The Business Change Manager/s is there to assist the Programme Director and Programme Manager in making the required changes to the organisation that will provide the benefits that the programme has been commissioned to achieve. Where a programme affects a large number of areas of the organisation it may be necessary to either appoint a number of managers to this role, or to put in place a structure which ensures that all the relevant managers are involved, for example a programme implementation group or committee.

Where the programme affects areas of the organisation that are controlled by different managers then it will be necessary to appoint managers from each of these areas to this role. (The exception to this is when one of these managers is given responsibility by the Sponsoring Group for all these areas for the duration of the programme).

The individual/s appointed to this role are the managers of the areas affected by the programme that have on going responsibility for that area. Where the programme is to put in place new products or services, or where the final manager of that area is not in place, the Business Change Manager may well be an interim manager who hands over to the permanent manager at the end of the programme.

Some of the specific activities that the Business Change Managers must perform are:

- ensure the programme meets the Sponsoring Groups requirements;
- work with the Programme Director and Programme Manager to deliver and sustain the defined benefits for the areas that they are responsible for;
- work with the Programme Manager to identify how the benefits will be realised and sustained;
- work with the Programme Manager to ensure that the portfolio of projects, initiatives or work packages that the programme contains will provide the ability to deliver the required programme benefits;
- assist the Programme Manager to identify benefits that may be common to more than one programme;
- assist the Programme Manager in identifying any duplicated activities that may exist in the portfolio in respect of realising benefits;

- plan and implement any preparatory work needed to ensure the areas that they are responsible for are prepared to deal with any revised business process or ways of working that are required to achieve the defined benefits;
- establish the way that the benefits will be delivered and how the impact of these benefits can be assessed;
- ensure that as the projects, initiatives or work packages are delivered the business areas achieve the planned improvements in new or existing business processes;
- lead all the activities needed to achieve the benefits and ensure that activities are in place to ensure sustainability.

The Business Change Manager/s work closely with both the Programme Director and the Programme Managers and have specific responsibility later in the programme for reporting the outcomes of the programme as compared to the programme's Blueprint and its Business Case.

The most important of the specific attributes required of the manager/s appointed to this role is a detailed knowledge of the business environment, processes, and culture of that part of the organisation involved in the programme.

The Business Change Manager must also have both the authority and management skills to "sell" the programme to the staff affected by the programme. Also to have the experience and general management skills to bring order to complex situations whilst keeping the Blueprint and the *Vision* it contains to the forefront.

The typical skills of the Business Change Managers are:

- detailed knowledge of the business environment;
- direct business area experience;

- an understanding of the programme and the concepts of programme management;
- an understanding of the management structures and culture of the organisation;
- management skills to co-ordinate programme personnel from different disciplines and differing viewpoints;
- effective marketing and communication skills;
- the ability to bring order and structure to complex situations
- ability to keep the programme objectives in focus and vision to the forefront;
- experience of Business Change and Management techniques;
- Business Process Re-engineering;
- Benefits Identification and Management Techniques.

As the programme is executed the Business Change Manager/s must take responsibility for monitoring the outcome of the programme as compared to that predicted in the Business Case and the Benefits Profile. Also, at specific defined points in the programme such as the end of a Tranche, to not only assess the plan for realising and sustaining the benefits they must also confirm that the programme is still viable.

3.6   Other Possible Roles

In addition to the Sponsoring Group, Programme Director and the Programme Manager it may well be advantageous to consider creating other roles to support the management of the programme.

These roles can be subdivided into two groups i.e those that primarily assist the Sponsoring Group and Programme Director and those that assist the Programme Manager.

Some of the roles described below however can assist both groups.

3.6.1 Support to the Sponsoring Group and the Programme Director.

The major requirements for additional roles to support the Sponsoring Group and the Programme Director is Programme Assurance.

The purpose of this role is to provide the Sponsoring Group, Programme Director or other key stakeholders in the programme, that the programme is:

1. Being managed appropriately;
2. The relevant process and procedures and standards are being followed;
3. The rationale for the programme is sound;
4. The programmes objectives and benefits are realistic and attainable.

When considering appointing or establishing these roles consideration must be given to:

- what is to be assured – the programme management processes and or the content of the programme?
- what skills and experience are required to undertake the programme assurance role?
- is the assurance to be provided for the programme as a whole and for the constituent projects, initiatives and work packages?
- what outputs are required from programme assurance and when?
- how will the assurance function keep abreast of the changes to the environment and business influences that the programme seeks to operate within?

In addition to these internal reasons for programme assurance there may well be other external requirements for programme assurance. For example in 2000 the UK Government introduced a system of "Gateway Review" for major programmes and projects in government departments. This "Gateway Review" required that each programme or project was assessed at predetermined intervals by an external group to ensure that the programme and the way that it was being managed was going to meet the organisations needs.

It would be wholly appropriate to consider incorporating the need for this type of assurance within the requirements for Programme Assurance, perhaps even amalgamating the two assurance roles into one function.

3.6.2 Support to the Programme Manager

There are two areas where the Programme Manager may require support – the first is with the design and assurance activities and the second, with the management of the programme itself.

The additional support in respect of the design and assurance activities are really delegations of the Programme Managers responsibilities to named individuals. Typically these appointments are made in respect of:

- *Design Authority – Preparing the strategic design for the systems or process or products that the programme is to deliver.

- **Technical Design* - This person(s) is usually a senior manager in the organisation. The role is to ensure that business processes still conform to the relevant standards, codes of practice, or agreed technical strategy following any changes made as a result of the programme.

- Compliance Management – Ensuring the programme and project management process are operating as agreed.

- Quality Assurance – ensuring that a consistent and cohesive strategy and tactical plans are in place to ensure the constituent portfolio of projects, initiatives and work packages meet the programmes quality policy and objectives.

*Note1: In the OGC's most recent advice the Design Authority role typically reports to the Programme Manager. This is because the types of programmes performed in government normally do not involve such major changes that require the most senior managers to be involved in assuring that the changes conform to relevant standards – however in commercial organisations the changes made by a programme may be so substantial as to demand that the manager allocated to this role is a senior or executive manager

**Note2: It is often found that the responsibility for this role could be spread over a number of managers. If so then it is important that all aspects of this role in the programme are allocated to the appropriate manager/s. This role is particularly important in the definition and identification phases of the programme.

The second area is that of management of the programme - For most programmes it is worth establishing either a Programme Support Office or a programme support function within the programme team. The choice of which of these options should be adopted will depend on the number of programmes that the organisation has operating at any one time and the likelihood that the use of programme management is to be permanent feature in the organisation.

The specific responsibility allocated to the Programme Support Office will depend on the skills and availability of appropriate resources as well as the need of the specific programme/s.

In addition to the typical activities listed below, the Programme Support Office may also be given responsibility for supplying advice and consultancy support to the Programme and Project Managers and the custodian of the programme management function and processes.

Some of the more common or typical tasks allocated to the Programme Support Office are:

- develop and maintain the overall Vision, Blueprint and integrated plan on behalf of the Programme Director;
- monitor progress of the integrated plan against the Blueprint, and ensure integration and review progress across the programmes;
- develop programme management frameworks, disciplines and knowledge;
- maintain the supporting standards and processes needed by Programme Managers;
- provide advice and support to delivery programmes.

Also optionally responsible for providing programme management support to individual Programme Managers in the following areas:

- risk management;
- programme planning;
- programme issues processes;
- progress reporting;
- confirming interfaces between programmes;
- supporting maintenance of the Programme Definition;
- advice and guidance on programme management processes.

3.7   Project Managers

The role of the Project Manager is usually defined by the project management method. The deployment of programme management does not materially change their role and responsibilities, however, it does add to or modify these in respect of the relationship between the project and the programme. For example the Project Manager's duties must now include:

- delivery of the specific project as defined by the Programme Plan;
- ensuring that the project is kept in alignment with the programme's objectives.

There will also be a need to amend the projects progress monitoring and reporting processes to ensure that they work in conjunction with those used at programme level.

3.8 Tailoring the Organisation Structure

The organisation structure defined in the *Programme Managers Companion* is designed to meet the needs of the average programme in the average organisation – therefore they will need to be adapted to suit different interests and needs of a particular programme.

On large or very complex programmes the management organisation structure may well need to be scaled up to meet the requirements for the programme and/or increase the need to appoint additional roles such as communications manager, risk manager, programme accountant, etc.

What is vital is that the need for clear direction and management is maintained – it is all too easy to make the structure so complicated that the clear direction and management becomes impossible.

Experience has shown that increasing the number of managers does not always improve the management of the programme – in fact quite often it does the reverse. Tailoring of the structure must therefore be done judiciously and only after careful consideration of the consequences.

SECTION FOUR: PROGRAMME IDENTIFICATION

4.1 The Start Point – The Strategic Goals and Business Plan

In most organisations, at the start of the business planning cycle the Board holds an annual workshop(s) to identify it's Strategic Goals and short term Business Goals or Objectives. This is developed into the Business Plan.

As part of the annual planning process the Sponsoring Group reviews the programmes and projects that they are responsible for to ensure that delivery of these programmes and projects will achieve the Strategic Goals, the Business Goals and objectives. If the need for a new programme or project is identified then they must prepare a Programme Mandate or Project Mandate.

The Programme Mandate is the start of the programme and triggers the start of this process.

The Programme Mandate is a short document, which contains at least the following information:

- What the programme is to deliver in terms of new services/products or operational capacity;
- how the organisation will be improved (or improved benchmarks) as a result of what the programme is to deliver;
- how the programme fits into the Strategy or Business Goals of the organisation;
- any related or interdependent programmes or initiatives that are underway or will be commissioned during the programme.

4.2   Introduction and Purpose of this Process

This process and the first phase of the programme identifies the outline scope of the programme and documents this in the form of a Programme Brief.

This process is nearly always an integral part of the organisation's business planning and management processes. The organisation's business planning/strategy development process identifies any gaps in the activities and hence the need to commission a programme of activity. Programmes must align with the business strategy as described in the business plan.

Where relevant, reference to these processes have been included in this section of the *Programme Managers Companion* to ensure that the Programme Manager understands how the need for the programme arose and the process that led to its commissioning.

This process ensures that the Programme Director and Programme Manager have sufficient information upon which to develop a Programme Brief which will be used firstly, to confirm with the Sponsoring Group that the programme will meet their requirements and secondly, to provide the information required in the next process to enable the Programme Director and Programme Manager to develop and agree the Programme Definition and associated Project Mandates/Briefs.

4.3   Programme Vision

The Programme Director then prepares the first two sections of the Programme Blueprint – the Vision statements. The term Blueprint is used to describe the totality of the changes being made by the programme to support the Business Strategy and Plan.

The Programme Director will be supported during this process by members of staff who assist the Programme Director. In some organisations the Programme Manager may well lead this process.

The Programme Blueprint contains four sections:

- Business Vision -the benefits to the organisation (including the measures) that the programme is designed to achieve;
- Operational Vision -the way the organisation will operate when the programme has been completed;
- Culture and/or Attitude Change Plan;
- Communication Plan.

It is vital that these "Visions" are fully understood and agreed by the organisation particularly by the Programme Director and the members of the Sponsoring Group. A good way to achieve this understanding is for the Programme Director or Manager to arrange a series of workshops or meetings at which these aspects of the programme are discussed – or demonstrated, before they are formally documented and agreed.

It is important to remember that at this early stage of the programme it is likely that these definitions will not be fully defined – they will however be regularly reviewed during the programme and refined as the uncertainties associated with the programme are resolved.

4.4   Programme Brief

The Programme Director or Programme Manager, produces the Programme Brief for presentation to and agreement by the Sponsoring Group, before the programme proceeds to its Definition Phase.

The Programme Brief will contain:

- Background to the programme and how it relates to or supports the Strategy and or Business Goals;
- The Vision Statement – a description of the Business and Operational Vision that the programme is designed to achieve;
- Known risks;
- High level estimates of the overall effort required to deliver the programme.

4.5   The Plan for defining the Programme Process

The Programme Director and his team or Programme Manager prepares a plan of the activities that will be needed to complete the Programme Definition process. This will take account of all the activities needed to prepare and agree the constituent document with the relevant members of the organisation.

4.6   The appointment of the members of the Programme Organisation Structure

At this stage of the programme a number of appointments may be made to the programme's organisation structure – the mandatory roles that must be allocated and formal appointments made are the Programme Director and the Programme Manager. Other roles may be decided and appointed at this point or at the end of the Definition process (see section 3 of the *Programme Managers Companion*)

4.7   Approval to proceed

Once the Programme Brief and all the other components of this process have been completed then the Programme Director presents the documents to the Sponsoring Group and asks for their formal approval to proceed to the Programme Definition process.

4.8   Checklist

Action	Output
1. The Business Planning Team are responsible for preparing the Business Plan and Strategy on behalf of the organisation.	Business Plan and Strategy
2. The Sponsoring Group identifies if a new or amended programme is needed to fulfil the Business Strategy and Business Plan and prepares the Programme Mandate.	Programme Mandate
3. Using the Programme Mandate and the Business Strategy and Plan, the Programme Director or Programme Manager prepares the first two sections of the Programme Blueprint – the Vision Statements) – this must be approved by the Programme Director and/or the Sponsoring Group).	Part of the Programme Blueprint the: Business Vision Operational Vision Programme Brief
4. The Programme Director or Programme Manager establishes the programme management organisation structure (approved by the Sponsoring Group).	Programme Management: Organisation Roles Responsibilities
5. The Programme Director or Programme Manager prepares the plan for the Programme Definition process. (Approved by the Programme Director and or Sponsoring Group).	Programme Definition process plan
6. Approval to proceed with Programme Definition is obtained from the Sponsoring Group	Formal commitment and documentation of the approval to proceed.

SECTION FIVE: PROGRAMME DEFINITION

5.1   Introduction and purpose of this Process

This process confirms the detailed scope, objectives and plans and provides the foundation for the successful delivery of the programme. During this process a Programme Plan and Programme Definition (PD), which builds upon the Programme Brief, are developed.

The Programme Definition assures the Sponsoring Group and the Programme Director that the programme can meet its objectives. The potential implementation options that could be used to deliver the programme are examined and one selected that matches the required Benefits Realisation Profile (at an acceptable level of risk). A definition of the projects that will be needed to deliver the programme is identified and their specific contribution to the attainment of the programme's objectives agreed.

A Programme Plan is developed to match the agreed Benefits Realisation Profile. This information is used to develop the Programme Definition and the Project Mandates and Project Brief for the supporting projects.

5.2   Establish the Programme Definition team

The Programme Director usually requires other members of staff to assist with the definition of the programme – it is common for the Programme Manager (if one has been appointed) to take the lead in this component of the definition process.   The skills needed to prepare the Programme Definition are wide and include Strategic and Tactical Business Planning – Financial Investment Planning and, in-depth knowledge of the organisations management structure and business management processes.

It is again not uncommon for this team to consist of a number of the members of the organisation who will eventually be part of the formal

Programme Managers Companion

33

programme organisation structure. Each member of this team must have a defined role and be selected for their expertise and knowledge and not just because of their position or seniority in the organisation.

5.3 Complete the Blueprint

The Visions contained in the Programme Brief are now refined, updated and expanded into the full Blueprint for the programme

Typically the Blueprint contains the following sections:

Business Vision – a model of the functions, processes and decision-making operations that will be affected by the programme's deliverables.

This will be quantified with relevant changes in benchmarks or other performance measures that the programme is designed to achieve.

Operational Vision – a model of the impact that the programme's deliverables will have on the operation of the organisation including its structure and staffing levels and skills, culture and attitudes.

Infrastructure Requirements – The Information Systems and other facilities and tools that will be required to deliver or support the changes to made by the programme. The support and other services that will be required to support the deliverables from the programme and to ensure that the benefits achieve are sustained.

It is vital that these Vision statements are business focused and expressed in terms of what the programme is to achieve – not how it is to be done. – Failure to define these visions in business terms will severely inhibit the definition of real programme implentation options later in the definition process.

Stakeholder Identification and Analysis, the Change Plan

This important component of the Blueprint may in some programmes be large or important enough to be a component in its own right rather than an adjunct to the Blueprint.

This analysis identifies the groups of staff and others affected by, or who can effect, the success of the programme. The constituent members of these groups are defined and also their role in the success of the programme.

Such names as Change Leaders, Change Agents, Participants, Bystanders, Ambassadors are often used to define the role of these groups. This definition is then used to define what changes in attitude or culture will be needed from each of these groups in order for the programme to be a success.

This Change Plan will provide the basis of other components of this process including the Communication Strategy and Plan. This Change Plan can in some programmes contribute a large proportion of the benefits that the programme is designed to provide.

Communication Strategy and Plan

As with the Change Plan this component may either be found in the Blueprint or, if this aspect is important enough, treated as separate component of this process.

This strategy and the plan must define the information that is to flow out and into the programme. These flows are often shown in relation to the groups defined in the Change Plan.

The Communication Plan must define what information is to be provided to who; by what means; at what time intervals; or events in the programme.

5.4   Investment/Benefits Appraisal

The main purpose of the Programme Definition process in a programme is to define what and how much, benefit is to be obtained from the programme and to agree the budget for the programme.

This is then discussed with the Programme Director and the Benefits Realisation Profile – (what benefits and costs must be achieved and spent by when) agreed.

Based on these high level definitions the Programme Manager will develop and agree the Benefits Realisation Profile and then the possible programme implementation options.

These options will then be presented to the Programme Director and the Sponsoring Group and their decision sought as to which option the programme should follow.

Based on this agreed option and the Benefits Realisation Profile and high level costs and benefits, the Programme Manager can define the portfolio of projects, initiatives and work packages that will be needed to deliver the programme.

The Investment Appraisal for a programme starts with the definition and measurement of the potential benefits that will be provided by the programme. This is usually derived from the Business Vision section of the Programme Blueprint.

Having identified the potential benefits the assessment of how much should, or could, be invested by the organisation to achieve those benefits needs to be determined. The amount of the investment should ideally be decided before the identification of the detailed implementation options.

This approach is recommended to ensure:

- the amount allocated to the programme is based on its value or worth to the organisation; and,
- the projects are designed to be within that cost – not the other way round!

The organisation may be prepared to invest only a small proportion of the projected benefits on the programme if they are not certain that the function will continue to be required in the near future – or perhaps multiples of the savings if they believe the function will continue for many years.

5.5   Implementation Options

Having determined how much money and other resources are available to invest in the programme the Programme Manager develops the implementation options that could be used to implement the requirements of the programme.

These implementation options must provide benefits that match the required Benefits Realisation Profile. As a consequence, it may be necessary to propose options which concentrate on delivering benefits as early as possible. To do this it may sometimes be prudent to commission projects that may look "illogical", in that they may not represent the most efficient method of delivering the project, but will deliver the programme benefits earlier than alternative options.

This is perfectly acceptable providing the costs of these "illogical" sequence options remain within that agreed in the Investment Appraisal.

It is important that the implementation options considered are truly independent options not just subsets of the same one.

For example if the programme is to reduce the cost of the invoice system the options defined in the document could well be:

1. Review existing paperwork systems and processes and improve them empirically.
2. Carry out Business Process Re-engineering (supported by a new IT system) of the whole invoice process.
3. Subcontract invoice generation to an external organisation.

These options should be presented with a recommendation to the Programme Director and the Sponsoring Group for a decision.

This process refines the Operational Vision contained in the Programme Blueprint and also helps ensure that the Programme Director and the Sponsoring Group do not have any mis-understandings of what the programme is to achieve.

The implementation options report also contains an analysis of the risk of each option and an indication of the possible tranches and milestones in the programme.

These options are supported by the Initial Programme Plans, which the Programme Manager prepares for each of the options. These Initial Programme Plans are only a high level plan and resource requirement specification.

Supporting these Programme Plans is either a graph or table, which describes the Benefits Realisation Profile of each of these options. (This Benefits Realisation Profile describes what and when; the benefits that would be achieved). It is usually found that the Profiles show the three "classic" profiles of 'Benefits Early', 'Benefits Medium Term', and 'Benefits Long Term'.

The completed report is then passed to the Programme Director and Sponsoring Group for a decision on which option (and Benefits Realisation Profile) they wish to adopt. The Programme Manager should make a recommendation as to which option is preferred.

Each option is typically evaluated with the following criteria:

- does it propose a solution that fits the aim and objectives of the programme?
- does it provide cost effective and cost efficient benefits to the organisation?
- does it provide the required benefits in the required timescales?
- can it be completed in the required timescales?
- can it be developed using available resources?
- are the risks to the business and the programme manageable?

5.6   Quality Management Strategy

The Programme Manager and Programme Director define the required Quality Strategy for the programme. This strategy must take into account the nature of the programme and the decisions that have been made in terms of its benefits and costs. For example, if this programme is directed towards quick wins and has a short life expectancy – then the Quality Strategy will reflect that by perhaps only setting out to prepare some of the deliverables and work packages to defined quality standards.

This Quality Strategy should also include the arrangements made for Programme Assurance either by internal or external teams.

5.7   Risk Management Strategy and Initial Risk Log

The Programme Director and the Programme Manager discuss and agree how risks to the programme will be identified, assessed, contained and, managing actions decided, monitored and controlled.

This strategy should also include the interface and relationship between the programme and the constituent projects, initiatives and work packages and how risks will be passed between them.

Included in this strategy is the implementation of the Risk Registers or Log at both programme and project levels.

5.8 Project – Programme Contribution Matrix

Having agreed which of the implementation options is to be used for the programme, the Programme Manager then refines the initial Programme Plan into the first formal Programme Plan. The first part of this is the preparation of the 'Project – Programme Contribution Matrix'.

Experience, in other organisations, has shown that an effective way to do this is to convene a Programme Initiation Workshop which is attended by the prospective Project Managers of the projects likely to constitute the programme.

The discussions are summarised onto the Project – Programme Contribution Matrix. At this stage this matrix contains the list of new or existing projects initiatives and work packages and a definition of their aim, objectives, scope and major deliverables.

If the matrix contains existing projects or programmes that are being subsumed into a new programme, it is vital to identify any differences between the requirements needed for this new programme and what the projects are currently tasked to deliver. Any differences need to be investigated and control action exercised as appropriate.

It is important to note that in some instances a project can be contributing to more than one programme. In such circumstances it is vital that any realignment of the project is carried out in consultation with all the Programme Managers who utilise the deliverables from the project.

Having identified the list of projects the Programme Manager must then define and obtain agreement from the Programme Director of the percentage contribution that each of these projects or initiatives will make to the attainment of the programme's goals and benefits.

This allocation can be made on the basis of:

- monetary benefits;
- other quantitative benefits (e.g. delivery of x);
- qualitative benefits (e.g. cultural changes);
- must, should or could criteria;
- weighting and ranking by importance.

The method(s) used to assess the contribution made should be tailored to meet the individual programme needs, but it is vital that the contribution percentage is agreed with the Programme Director.

Note: It is normal practice for the organisation to allow the Programme Director to authorise the inclusion of new scoping projects into the programme.

However before any such project moves into implementation phase it will need to be approved by the organisations project authorisation and resource prioritisation process.

5.9   Programme Plan

The Programme Manager prepares the first formal Programme Plan so that it matches the agreed Benefits Realisation Profile. This is achieved by scheduling the projects by using the contribution they provide. This is normally produced in the form of a Gantt chart and supporting explanatory narrative.

Any logical anomalies that emerge as a result of scheduling the projects in this way must be resolved before this plan is presented to the Programme Director for approval. It is often found that when such anomalies emerge it is necessary to restructure projects or define new or different projects in order to remedy problems.

Therefore it is recommended that the Programme Director is not asked to formally agree the contribution percentages (see previous paragraphs) until the Programme Manager is reasonably certain that the list of projects etc. is correct.

In designing this Programme Plan the Programme Manager uses the Required Benefits Profile to help identify the potential "Islands of Stability" and the accompanying programme Tranches. Tranches are divisions of the programme. They represent points in the programme where clearly defined changes have been achieved - thus presenting an Island of Stability. This gives the opportunity to review what the programme has achieved, what is left to achieve and to reassess the viability of the remainder and direction of the programme.

The position of these programme review points are decided after considering a number of a factors:

- where major benefits are achieved;
- where major commitments in respect of resources, costs or other commitments are made;
- where major parts of the programme have been delivered;
- major events external to the programme that effect it (i.e. the annual budgeting/planning process).

Before this plan is "published" the Programme Manager should convene a workshop with the relevant Project Managers to identify the major interdependencies that exist between the projects (and with other programmes) that are important to the programme.

The Programme Manager should ensure the relevant Project Managers have plans and Product Descriptions in place so that these projects do successfully interface.

The Programme Plan also includes the policy and arrangements the Programme Manager has set in place as regards the quality and change control regimes to be used.

Typically these elements of the Programme Plan define who has responsibilities for which parts of these processes, how the processes are to be operated and the standards that are to be applied.

5.10 Benefits Management and Realisation Plans

The Benefits Management Plan explains the arrangements that have and will be put into place to define, realise, and sustain the benefits that the programme is designed to achieve.

This plan is normally developed by the Business Change Manager and the Programme Manager and Programme Director.

Having defined the Programme Plan the Programme Manager will then develop the Benefits Realisation Plan. At this stage the plan contains the areas of benefits and the names of the managers who will be involved in implementing the actions needed to realise the programme benefits and to ensure that these benefits are sustained. The actions that will be used to realise and sustain the benefits should be included within the Programme Plan.

5.11   Finalise the Programme Management Organisation Structure

The Programme Director and the Programme Manager then complete the definition of the programme management organisation structure. This must contain each of the primary roles and also any additional roles that have been deployed for this programme.   It is useful to include a short explanation of the reason for the allocation of the members of staff to that role and in particular any additional roles that have been created.

This should also include a definition of the role and any specific terms of reference that have been agreed with the role post holder.

5.12   Programme Definition

The Programme Manager and the Programme Director and perhaps assisted by the Programme Support Office, develop the Programme Definition (PD) using the organisation' current standard template document. This document provides the baseline for the programme. The Programme Definition is a 'living document' and should be updated regularly throughout the life of the programme to always contain an accurate reflection of the current position of the programme.

The Programme Definition typically contains the following information.

- Programme Blueprint (including Change Plan and Communications Strategy and Plan);
- Required Benefits Profile;
- Benefits Realisation Plan;
- Agreed implementation options (Method of Approach);
- Programme Management Organisation Structure;
- Programme Plan (including Tranches and narrative);
- Business Case;
- Resource & finance requirements;
- Quality Management Strategy;

Programme Managers Companion

44

- Risk Analysis;
- List of constituent projects; initiatives and work packages;
- Programme Communication Plan;
- Project – Programme Contribution Matrix.

The document is usually prepared in sections and informally agreed with the Programme Director prior to the formal acceptance meeting and presentation to the Sponsoring Group for their approval. This helps to ensure that any minor questions raised are dealt with in advance and therefore avoids an overlong meeting. The Programme Definition should be compared with the documents prepared in the Programme Identification Process/Phase to ensure that it is still within the scope and limits of those documents. Any significant variance must be discussed with the Sponsoring Group and appropriate action taken.

5.13 Project Start up and Initiation Documents

Once the Sponsoring Group has approved the Programme Definition (PD) the Programme Manager and the Project Managers ensure that up to date Project Start up (Project Mandate and Project Brief) and or Project Initiation Documents (PIDs) exist for all the projects within the programme.

If any of the existing projects which are being subsumed into the programme need to be realigned then the Programme Manager must discuss this with the relevant Project Manager (and Project Board to ensure that they understand what is required of them and that the project will be within the agreed scope and framework). It is quite common for substantial changes to be required in such existing projects. In some cases it is necessary to put the project on hold until it can be realigned.

5.14   Checklist

Action	Outputs
1. Establish the Programme Definition Team.	
2. Complete the Programme Blueprint (approved by the Programme Director and the Sponsoring Group).	Programme Blueprint
3. The Programme Manager prepares the Investment Appraisal of the programme (approved by the Programme Director and the Sponsoring Group).	Investment Appraisal Required Benefits Profile
4. The Programme Manager prepares the Programme implementation options report (the Programme Director and Sponsoring Group decide which option should be adopted).	Programme implementation options report
5. The Programme Manager together with the potential Project Managers identifies the candidate projects and agrees the Project – Programme Contribution Matrix.	Project- Programme Contribution Matrix
6. The Programme Manager prepares the remainder of the Programme Plan.	Programme Plan: Programme Plan Description Programme processes for progress monitoring & reporting Change Control
7. The Programme Manager prepares the Benefits Management Strategy and the Benefits Realisation Plan to include owners and actions.	Benefits Management Strategy and Benefit Realisation Plan
8. Programme Manager and Programme Director define and agree the Programme Management Organisation Structure.	Programme organisation structure roles and responsibilities
9. Programme Manager and Programme Director define and agree the Quality Management Strategy.	Programme Quality Management Strategy
10. Programme Manager and Programme Director define and agree the Risk Management and Initial Risk Log.	Risk Strategy and Risk Log
11. The Programme Manager prepares the Programme Definition (approved by the Programme Director and the Sponsoring Group).	Programme Definition
12. Programme Manager and the Project Managers complete Project Start Up or Project Initiation Documents (approved by Programme Manager) .	Project Mandate or Brief or Project Initiation Documents (PIDs)

Programme Managers Companion

SECTION SIX: MANAGING THE PROGRAMME AND PROJECT PORTFOLIO – MONITORING AND CONTROL

6.1 Introduction and Purpose of these Processes

The OGC guidance entitled "Managing Successful Programmes" uses three processes to cover the Establishing (setting up), Managing the Project Portfolio (implementation of the programme) and Delivering Benefit. These are not usually followed sequentially in a programme but are "mixed and matched" together during the implementation or delivery of the programme.

As all three of these processes are used during the implementation of a Tranche they have been integrated together in this section of the *Programme Managers Companion* so that the Programme Manager can see the three processes as a whole.

6.1 Establish the Programme

This process is carried out at the start of the programme – it is also advisable to repeat this process at the end of each of the programmes Tranches to ensure the arrangements that were put in place at the start of the programme are still relevant and are operating as they were intended. If not then control action is required.

6.1.1 Set-up the Programme Organisation Structure

This component of the process consists of setting up and putting in place the arrangements that have been defined for the organisation structure that is to support the management of the programme.

This will involve ensuring that the members of staff who have been allocated a role and responsibilities understand that role and that they receive any required training needed to carry out their roles and responsibilities.

Programme Managers Companion

47

The major effort required however is setting up the programme support arrangements – particularly if a Programme Support Office is to be established.

The Programme Manager must ensure that adequate and efficient support arrangements are in place, especially in respect of programme documentation management and providing management information to monitor the progress made with the implementation of the programme.

6.1.2 Set-up the Processes and Procedures required to manage the programme

Having initiated the programme in a controlled and structured way it is essential that it remains under control by using a structured approach to monitoring and control.

This phase contains the mechanisms and processes that monitor the progress made in the projects and the programme and puts into action any control measures that are required. It also includes the regular updating of the Programme Plan and dealing with the day to day management of the programme including Issues Management, Risk Management and Change Control.

It is important that the following aspects of the management of the programme are put in place:

- Planning, tracking and reporting standards and procedures;
- Configuration management arrangements;
- Change Control processes and procedures;
- Issue Management processes and procedures;
- Quality Management planning and management;
- Risk identification, assessments action planning and action monitoring.

The effective monitoring of the progress made with the programme is essential if the organisation is to be able to exercise control during its implementation. It is essential that this monitoring looks at not only the progress made in executing the programme but also that the reasons for the programme are still valid. As a consequence the Programme Manager may have to put in place mechanisms to track the changes in benchmarks that the programme is to achieve – these benchmarks may include both business processes or performance related changes as well as culture or attitude.

Of equal importance is to define and agree the format of the progress reports that are to be provided from the programme. Failure to deal with this before the programme starts will lead to considerable effort being expended and wasted later in the programme when it is realised that without these having been defined and agreed, the Programme Manager will not know what information is to be collected by the programme to provide progress reports.

This typically results in <u>too much data and no information</u> being provided to those who need progress reports.

6.1.3 Define the standards and policies that will be used to manage the programme

It may also be necessary to prepare a list of the other related policies and standards that the programme will operate within. These other standards include:

- Human resource management policies
- Technology and other policies and strategies
- Procurement and contract management rules and standards
- Business practices and ethics

Programme Managers Companion

This monitoring must enable the organisation to identify when problems have occurred during that implementation process which are so serious that it needs to consider taking control action to regain control of the situation.

6.1.4 Set-up Benefits Measurement Process

The Programme Manager will have designed the programme to match the Required Benefit Realisation Profile – what is needed is to put in place arrangements to measure the attainment of these benefits.

Some of these may already be in place as part of the organisation's management process – perhaps as part of the Management Information System – however it is vital to assess whether these existing mechanisms will meet the requirements for monitoring the benefits to be attained.

One particular problem that may be experienced in using existing systems is the concept of "Benchmark Lag" this is where the Management Information Systems or Benchmarks lag behind the changes i.e. they do not reflect the changes that have been achieved. A classic example of this is the organisation's head count figures – quite often as staff have retired or been released it is several months before the head count figure actually reflects that they have left – this is because quite often such staff are kept on the payroll for a period after they have officially left.

6.1.5 Set-up the infrastructure and tools need to manage the programme

In some organisations this component can be omitted because they are provided – however even when they are provided it is still worth considering whether the standard infrastructure and tools will meet the requirements of this specific programme.

This infrastructure and tools may involve such things as web sites and other communication mediums, planning and scheduling tools, risk assessment tools etc.

6.1.6 Set-up the communication channels

This component may in some ways overlap some of the other components already described in this process. It uses the Communication Strategy and Plan and the Change Plan to define the mechanisms that will be required to ensure that the Communication Strategy and Change Plan can be implemented effectively and efficiently. It is important to note that at the start of each new Tranche the Change Plan and the Communication Strategy and Plan will need to be updated to reflect the changed roles that some of the stakeholder groups will take.

For example – Change Leaders early in the programme can become Change Ambassadors as the programme delivers the changes that they are to implement. Similarly participants in one Tranche may then become the Change Agents as the programme moves down into the day to day operation of the business processes that they control.

6.2   Managing the Project Portfolio and Delivering the Benefits

The programme delivers its benefits through the projects, initiatives and work packages that are contained within its portfolio.

This section of the *Programme Managers Companion* describes the components of the two processes defined in the OGC publication Managing Successful Programmes. In addition to these management processes, the OGC publication describes a number of techniques that are used to assist with management of the programme.

These are

- Programme Planning;
- Benefits Management;
- Stakeholder Management;
- Issue Management and Risk Management;
- Quality Management;
- Configuration Management;
- Audit.

To ensure that the Programme Manager sees the entirety of activities required to manage the implementation of the programme, this section includes the activities from these techniques that need to be addressed in the typical programme.

As with all such guidance this may need to be adjusted to reflect the needs of a specific organisation or programme.

6.2.1 As required – project or initiative or work package start-up

As defined in the Programme Plan, the Programme Manager will need to ensure that the projects, initiatives and work packages that comprise the programme portfolio are started up according to the organisation's commissioning processes.

The definitions of what these projects, initiatives and work packages are to consist of will come primarily from the Project to programme contribution matrix described in the previous section.

This will be supplemented by the relevant parts of the Investment Appraisal or the Benefits Realisation Profile.

In addition, this start-up information should be supplemented with information from the Programme Plan which describes the interfaces and interdependencies with other parts of the portfolio. In particular, any "handshakes" that must occur with other parts of the portfolio if the programme is to achieve its targets.

6.3 Progress Monitoring

Progress made with the delivery of the programme is monitored in respect of – the projects, initiatives and work packages that were commissioned and also the benefits realised by what the programme is delivering.

It is vital that the arrangements for performing this monitoring are put in place before the programme starts. In order that the progress reporting arrangements are as efficient and effective as possible, it is important to agree what information is to be provided from this component to who and when and how.

In setting up and performing the progress monitoring, it is vital that the Programme Manager does not become a super Project Manager – the Project Managers must take and operate within their agreed areas of responsibility. The Programme Manager must therefore concentrate on those activities, which are of real significance to the programme. These are typically the interdependencies between the projects, initiatives and work packages in the portfolio and, of special importance, the "handshakes" between those that deliver the programme milestones or benefits release points.

However, the Programme Manager must also ensure that they are confident that the reports they are receiving are realistic and that the projects are progressing according to plan.

To obtain this assurance it is important that the Programme Manager defines and deploys appropriate monitoring measures – these may involve such measures as:

- Setting "Burn Rate" targets for the expenditure and deliverables for the projects;
- Monitoring completion dates and costs;
- Comparing estimates with actuals.

The information obtained from the project, initiatives and work packages needs to be supplemented with information regarding the delivery of benefits and or changes in culture or attitude. It is in some ways more important to monitor these rather then the progress made with the projects – all too often the Programme Manager becomes deliverable focussed rather than benefits focussed. As with the project, initiatives and work package monitoring, it is vital that the Programme Manager defines as early as possible not just the way that these items will be monitored, but also how progress made will be reported.

6.3.1 Refine and update the Programme Plan

Based on the information received during the progress-monitoring component, the Programme Manager supported as relevant by the Programme Support Office, updates the Programme Plan.

This should not be an onerous task if the Programme Plan has been created at the right level i.e. it should contain only those elements for the project, initiatives and work package plans that are significant to the programme as a whole.

Thus unless some serious calamity has occurred, the update of the Programme Plan should mainly consist of collecting and collating the information needed to summarise the progress and expenditure made with the programme.

6.3.2 Updating the Benefits Realisation and Sustainability Plan

As part of the progress monitoring the benefits realised – part or whole will need to be monitored. The Programme Manager therefore can update the Benefits Realisation Plan and Sustainability Plan to reflect the benefits realised and also any changes to the plan that the Business Change Manager believes are required. In order to do this, the Programme Manager and the Business Change Manager must meet on a regular basis to review the progress made and to update the Benefits Realisation Plan. This information is included in the regular progress monitoring report that is provided at monthly intervals and also in more detail at the End of Tranche review.

6.3.3 Quality Monitoring

During each of the Tranches, in addition to monitoring the progress made, the Programme Manager must also monitor the effectiveness of the Quality Management Strategy and Plan. This monitoring can be performed at two levels – these levels roughly corresponding to the types of approaches used in testing i.e. Black and White Box.

The Black Box approach to monitoring the effectiveness of the Quality Management Strategy and Plan is to examine the outputs from the Quality Management Processes and assess whether the process is operating correctly or not from the quality of the outputs.

The sorts of measures that can be adopted with this are – failure rates of products after adoption – failures noted at Quality Review – amount of rework required in each deliverable etc.

A White Box approach would be typically achieved through the conducting of a Quality Review audit – where the Strategy and Plan were examined in depth as are the arrangements that had been put into place to deliver them.

It is important that the Programme Manager discusses and agrees with the Programme Director the approach that is to be used and discusses the results (and the implications of those results) of the review.

6.3.4 Risk Management Monitoring

In a similar way to the Quality Management Strategy the Risk Management arrangements must also be regularly reviewed.

Having defined the programme risks as part of the Programme Identification and Definition, the Programme Manager must regularly review not only the risks but also more importantly the actions that have been commissioned to contain or manage them. It is often found that organisations are excellent at identifying and assessing risks – however they do not follow this through by:

- putting in place actions with which to contain or manage those risks and more importantly;
- putting in place arrangements to monitor that the actions have been carried out;
- assessing the success or otherwise of those actions.

The Programme Manager must therefore ensure that the monitoring of the programme also includes monitoring the progress made with the Risk Actions and also, when these Actions have been completed, their effectiveness or otherwise.

It is recommended that a report covering these aspects of the programme is included in the monthly progress report.

6.3.5 Issue and Change Control monitoring

The arrangements put in place to manage and control the Issues and Change requests raised during the programme must also be regularly reviewed to ensure that they are being effective and also that they are operating efficiently.

To this end the Programme Manager must also monitor the operation of these management systems – as with Quality Management, the Programme Manager can do this by either adopting a Black or White Box approach.

The Black Box approach would look primarily at the outputs of these management processes and assess their effectiveness through that mechanism. The types of outputs that are monitored are:

- the number of change requests or issues raised (very high or low numbers is a signal that there may be something wrong);
- the time taken to deal with the issues and changes;
- the impact of those changes or issues on the programme – (if the impact is great then it indicates that all the risks have not been identified and that the containment or management strategy may not be strong enough to deal with them).

The White Box approach would adopt a similar approach to that of a Quality Review where the procedures and processes currently used would be examined in depth.

6.3.6 Configuration Status monitoring

At a detailed level the Programme Manager must ensure that the programme documentation is under control and the Programme's Configuration Library is up to date and contains the correct versions. The most effective way of ensuring this is for the Programme Manager to perform a Configuration Audit on at least part of the Configuration Library on a regular basis.

Performing the Configuration Audit also checks to see if a number of other Programme Management mechanisms are operating effectively – these include the Quality Management Plan, the Change Control process and also parts of the planning process.

6.4 Monthly Reporting:

The Programme Manager needs to provide the Programme Director and the Sponsoring Group with a monthly report, which reflects the current situation.

This report ensures that the programme is regularly monitored and the Programme Director and the Sponsoring Group are fully aware of the current status of the programme.

The key information that should be included in this report is:

- progress against milestones and interdependencies;
- programme risks;
- expenditure £;
- financial benefits £;
- Non-financial benefits.

The Programme Manager should ensure collation of the information from the individual projects and preparation of a summary of the information for the Programme Director. The Programme Manager should complete a narrative on any particular areas that need special attention, or where a decision or action is required.

Other supporting documentation includes programme and project plans, risk registers, financial reports and any other relevant management information. Programme Risk Log and plans should be updated on a monthly basis and reviewed by the Programme Manager.

6.5   End of Tranche Review

Having commissioned the programme, the Programme Manager must ensure its progress is regularly reviewed by the Programme Director and the Sponsoring Group. This review includes the reasons that led to the programme being commissioned and the benefits that have been realised to date.

This major review occurs at the end of each Tranche because as the programme progresses, changes to the business environment may change. It is vital therefore to determine whether the reasons that led to the commissioning of the programme are still valid and the programme is moving in the correct direction.

The progress report prepared by the Programme Manager at the end of the Tranche and submitted to the Programme Director and the Sponsoring Group for consideration must therefore contain, in addition to the information provided in the monthly reports;

- progress and costs to date of the constituent projects;
- full details of benefits realised to date from the programme;
- changes to the business environment that have occurred from the baseline established in the strategic review;
- a current/up-dated copy of the Programme Definition; an up-dated copy of the Programme Plan.

The Programme Director or Sponsoring Group decides on any control action that is required in respect of:

- amendments to the existing projects and initiatives which make up the programme;
- declaring the programme complete or no longer valid;
- review of the programmes goals and objectives.

Programme Managers Companion

The timing of this review should be linked into one of the regular progress reports made to the organisation's Board, who should be asked to endorse the recommendations made by the Programme Director.

6.6 Exception Situation Reviews

If a project, which is either part of the programme, or affects part of the programme, raises an Exception Report, the Project Manager must send a copy of the report to the relevant Programme Manager(s). The Programme Manager(s) then evaluates the impact of the Exception Report on the programme. The Programme Support Office, relevant departmental manager and/or Project Manager can give assistance with this evaluation.

If the evaluation identifies that there will be a significant impact on the programme, the Programme Manager will discuss with the relevant Project Manager how to address the problem and whether the Exception Report will require a Programme Exception Plan to be developed. If this is the case the Programme Manager and the relevant Project Manager develop an Exception Report and present the situation to the Programme Director. The Programme Director then decides what action needs to be taken to deal with the situation.

6.7 Checklist

ACTION	OUTPUT
ESTABLISH THE PROGRAMME	
1. The Programme Manager and the Programme Director put in place the Programme Organisation Structure – i.e. Including the Programme Support Office.	Defined and agreed terms of reference and roles and responsibilities
2. The Programme Manager and the Programme Support Office put in place the processes and procedures to manage the programme.	Programme Management processes and procedures
3. The Programme Manager and the Programme Director ensure that the policies and standards the programme is to operate within are understood and defined.	List of defined standards and policies
4. The Programme Manager, Programme Director, Business Change Manager and the Programme Support Office put in place the arrangement to measure benefits provided by the programme.	Benefits measurement arrangements
5. The Programme Manager and the Programme Support Office set up the infrastructure and tools needed to manage the programme.	Programme Management Infrastructure and tools
6. The Programme Manager, Programme Director and the Programme Support Office put in place the communications channels.	Communication channels installed

Programme Managers Companion

MANAGING THE PORTFOLIO AND DELIVERING BENEFITS	
7. As required the Programme Manager and the Programme Director supported by the Project Support Office commission or start up projects, initiatives or work packages as required.	Projects, initiative or work package start up documents
8. The Programme Manager and the Programme Support Office operate the progress monitoring arrangements for both the delivery of the projects, initiatives and work packages and the benefits that they are to deliver.	Progress reports
9. The Programme Manager updates the Programme Plan to reflect the progress made.	Updated Programme Plan
10. The Programme Manager together with the Business Change Manager updates the Benefits Realisation and Sustainability Plan to reflect the progress made and changes to the Benefits Realisation Plan.	Updated Benefits Realisation and Sustainability Plan
11. The Programme Manager assesses the effectiveness of the Quality Management Strategy and Quality Management Plan.	Report on the effectiveness of the Quality Management arrangements and amendments as required.
12. The Programme Manager and the Programme Director review the effectiveness of the Risk Management process and assess the effectiveness of the Risk Actions that have been completed.	Updated Risk Log and Plan
13. The Programme Manager performs a partial Configuration Audit to ensure that the Configuration Management is working effectively.	Configuration/Status Report
14. **Monthly Monitoring:** Risk Register and Programme Plan updated by the Programme Manager and the Programme Support Office and reviewed by the Programme Director. The Programme Manager / Programme Support Office collates the project level reports and produces a programme level report. This report is reviewed by the Programme Director.	Updated Risk Register & Programme Plan Monthly Report
15. **End of Tranche Programme Reviews:** At the end of each programme Tranche the Programme Manager carries out a full review of the programme and its constituent projects. This report is approved by the Programme Director and the Sponsoring Group and if relevant the Board.	End of Tranche programme progress reports
16. **Exception Situation Review:** The Programme Manager prepares an Exception Report and Plan. The Programme Director reviews the report and agrees what actions should be taken.	Exception report and plan.

Programme Managers Companion

62

SECTION SEVEN: PROGRAMME CLOSURE

7.1   Introduction and purpose of this process

As the programme progresses there are number of reasons that may lead the Sponsoring Group to formally close the programme:

- the programme has been completed;
- the programme has achieved the required changes in business operations and/or practices;
- the programme has failed due to a problem that cannot be successfully addressed;
- the programme has to be cancelled because either the business environment has changed or the programme is no longer needed; or, the business can no longer resource the programme in its agreed form.

The Programme Closure process ensures that the programme is closed down in an orderly manner and:

- evaluates the success of the programme, the methods and procedures used to manage and execute it;
- ensures that the lessons learnt are captured for future programmes and projects;
- ensures that arrangements are put into place to manage the delivery of any benefits realisation actions that are outstanding; formally records the arrangements that have been put in place to ensure benefits are sustained.

7.2   End of programme documentation

The Programme Manager

- collects and collates the information contained in End Project Reports from those projects, subsumed within the programme that have been completed;
- collects and collates the current status reports from those projects that are still on-going;
- includes the project reports within the Programme Closure Report;
- ensures that any lessons learnt from an individual project are brought to the attention of the Programme Director. These should be divided into those which are specific to this programme and those of general interest to all programmes.

The Programme Manager prepares an update of the programme's Benefit Realisation and Sustainability Plan to show:

- what has been accomplished;
- what is left to be accomplished;
- who is responsible for the remainder of the plan;
- when the remaining elements will be completed.

Any changes to that plan, since the Programme Director and Sponsoring Group last saw it, should be highlighted (if significant changes have occurred then this should also be reported to the Board).

The Programme Manager must also prepare an update of the programme Investment Appraisal/Business Case, which details, the benefits that have been achieved e.g. a change in the relevant benchmark. In preparing this analysis the Programme Manager must ensure that any changes quoted in the report are accurate and also that any delays in the reduction of the benchmark, have been taken into account.

Any constituent projects that have not yet been completed should either be cancelled or subsumed into another programme (new or existing). Recommendations should be made in the final section of the Programme Closure Report.

7.3   Programme closure meeting

The Programme Manager arranges the Programme Closure Meeting with the Programme Director and Sponsoring Group. As with the end of Tranche reports it is advisable for the Programme Manager to discuss the contents of the report informally with the Programme Director prior to the meeting.

These discussions give the Programme Manager the opportunity to identify if the Programme Director will require any other members of either the programme or project management organisation structure to attend that meeting. At the meeting with the Sponsoring Group they review the report and then decide what follow on action will be needed in respect of:

- recommending to the Board that the programme is closed or not;
- recommending to the Board what should happen to any outstanding projects;
- identifying what follow on action should be taken regarding lessons learnt;
- The monitoring and control of the benefits realisation/sustainability plan.

The results of the programme closure meeting must be documented and turned into a paper for submission to the Board by the Programme Manager and the Programme Director. This paper should be a summary of the key contents of the Programme Managers Programme Closure Report and the decisions made at the meeting of the Sponsoring Group.

7.4 Closure communication

Following on from the approval of the Programme Closure Report, the Programme Manager must notify all the members of the Programme Management Team (including the individual Project Managers and Project Boards) that the programme is closed and, the arrangements agreed by the Sponsoring Group or Board for any outstanding or incomplete projects. The Programme Manager must ensure that all members of the organisation who need to be informed of the closure of the programme and the follow on arrangements are also notified. This should include closing down of the relevant budget codes. The Programme Manager must also ensure that individual projects have put into place a plan to deal with any outstanding activities.

7.5 Lessons learnt

The final step in the Programme Closure Process is to ensure all the lessons learnt that are relevant to future projects and programmes are passed to the relevant members of staff within the business and, to the Programme Support Office, to incorporate into the working practices and infrastructure for future programmes and projects. This should include recommended changes to procedures, standards or templates and also any information that has been acquired during the programme.

7.6   Checklist

ACTION	OUTPUT
1. The Programme Manager produces the Programme Closure Report and updates the Benefits Realisation and Sustainability Plan.	Programme Closure Report: -Updated Benefits Realisation and Sustainability Plan -Lessons Learnt.
2. The Programme Director approves the Programme Closure Report and agrees any following on action needed.	Programme Director meeting minutes
3. Following the approval by the Programme Director the Programme Manager and Programme Director present the Programme Closure report to the Sponsoring Group and agree any follow on actions.	
4. Following agreement of the Sponsoring Group to close the programme the Programme Manager and Programme Director prepare notifications that the programme has been completed.	Notifications to Line, Resource and Project Managers of programme closure
5. The Programme Manager ensures that the Programme Support Office updates the programme support framework and supporting infrastructure systems are updated as required.	Lessons learnt action report

Programme Managers Companion

SECTION EIGHT: GLOSSARY OF TERMS

TERM	DESCRIPTION
Blueprint	A description of all the changes that the delivery of the programme/s are designed to achieve, or a description of the organisation once the programme/s have been completed.
Integrated Plan	A series of documents which describes the schedule of major deliverables of the portfolio of programmes and projects, workpackages and other activities commissioned to achieve the Blueprint.
Programme Change Vision	A description of either, the changes that the delivery of a programme is designed to achieve, or a description of the organisation once the programme has been completed. (Can also be used in those situations where the realisation of the Blueprint has been subdivided between a number of programmes)
Operational Vision	A part of the Blueprint or Change Vision that describes the way that the organisation will operate after the portfolio, or single programme, has been completed.
Business Vision	A part of the Blueprint or Change Vision that describes the financial and other quantitative and qualitative changes that will occur in the organisation's operations, after a portfolio or single programme has been completed.

Programme Managers Companion

TERM	DESCRIPTION
Change Plan	A plan which describes for each of the relevant stakeholders the changes in their culture and/or attitude that are necessary to enable the portfolio or single programme to succeed, and the actions that will be used to achieve that change in culture and/or attitude.
Communication Plan	A plan which defines who will communicate with whom, about what and when, during the programme.
Implementation Options	The different methods of approach that could be deployed to execute the programme within the constraints of the agreed Investment Appraisal and will provide the Required Benefits Profile.
Required Benefits Profile	A document which describes what and how much of each benefit should be delivered, at what point in time.
Programme Definition	The document which defines the agreed baseline of the programme – including its aims and objectives, implementation plan, management arrangements and describes its constituent portfolio of projects work packages and other activities.
Project - Programme Contribution Matrix	A document which contains a list of the projects, initiatives, work packages and other activities in the programmes portfolio and the agreed estimation of their individual contribution to the aims and objectives of the programme.

TERM	DESCRIPTION
Programme Initiation Workshop	A workshop convened at the start of a programme to identify the projects, initiatives, work packages and other activities needed to deliver the programme's aims and objectives.
Grieving Cycle	The step changes in psychological attitude that all human beings experience when having to deal with changes.
Y Front approach	A diagram used to illustrate (and decide on) the typical actions needed to either obtain a persons commitment, or compliance to changes. (This is used in developing the Change Plan)
Portfolio	The term used to describe the collection of projects, initiatives, work packages and other activities commissioned to support
or	deliver a specific programme.

Note: The glossary may need to be revised to reflect any specific or additional terminology introduced by a specific organisation.

APPENDICES

Supporting Techniques

APPENDIX A: PREPARING THE CHANGE (CULTURE AND OR ATTITUDE) PLAN.

What must change

For a programme to be successful it is nearly always necessary for there to be some change in the culture or attitude of the staff affected by, or who will use, the new processes or technologies to be provided by the programme. A failure to recognise this fact and not to have included actions to achieve the required shift/s in culture/attitude can often negate a large part of the benefits that the programme is to achieve. This section of the programme Blueprint will describe at a high level any major cultural or attitude shifts that will be required to support the programme.

The following chart can be used to identify where (and possibly what) changes may be required. It is used by putting into the subject area box what supporting changes in culture or attitude are needed in respect of that defined subject area to facilitate a successful conclusion to the programme.

Supporting the Business & Operation Vision

External Environment

Mission/Strategy   Leadership   Culture

Structure   Management   Systems

Task and Skill Requirements   Work Unit Climate   Individual Needs and Values

Motivation

Individual/Organisational Performance

Programme Managers Companion

72

Who must change

Having identified in the previous section the areas of change that are needed in order to construct a Change (Culture and or Attitude) Plan it is then advisable to:

- identify the various groups of people affected by the programme;
- define their role in the programme and their attitude to the programme;
- decide what level of support is required from them if the programme is to be a success.

The next step is to identify the names of individuals or groups of people who constitute each of the groups shown below.

(It is vital to note that the allocation of these roles to a group of people does vary as the programme progresses. As a consequence, the plan that is put into place to affect or influence the attitude of these staff will also change as the programme progresses).

The Roles of the Staff Involved in the Changes

- **Ambassador**
  Supports, influences, advocate
- **Leader**
  Demands and authorises change
- **Agent**
  Responsible for achieving change
- **Participant**
  Must change for benefits to be obtained
- **Stakeholders/Bystander**
  Has a view does not participate or change

Programme Managers Companion

What must they change to

The major decision that has to be made is what type of support is required from that group for the programme to be a success and how to obtain that support.

For example if a group or individual cannot materially influence the programme or its success and their attitude at present (and when the programme is executed) is not particularly important, then obtaining their total 'buy in' to the programme is unnecessary. (Compliance will suffice.)

The 'Y front' approach illustrates this and helps in deciding the type and level of commitment required.

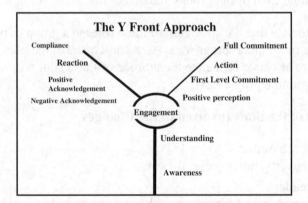

In deciding what tactics to use, the general rules are that to obtain commitment face to face consultation and communication is generally needed; whilst compliance can be achieved through more remote methods.

There are a number of 'influencers' which help build awareness. A number of effective influencing methods are indicated in the following list.

Tactics and Activities to Consider

- **Commitment (Requires Face to Face)**
  One to one meetings
- **Team meetings**
  Planning Workshops
- **Compliance**
  E Mail, letters, Videos, Audio Cassettes, Notice Boards, Memos
- **Influencers (Builds Awareness)**
  Road shows, Conferences.
  Training, Focus Groups, Briefing Groups

Helping them change

The construction of the Change (Culture and/or Attitude) Plan will need to take account of the changes in culture and/or attitudes that people go through when facing and experiencing major amendments or changes to their working and other environments.

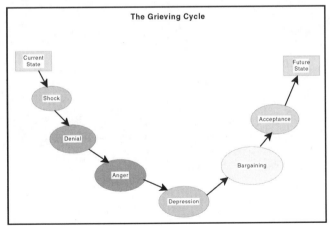

Programme Managers Companion

75

What is needed in preparing the Change (Culture and or Attitude) Plan is to recognise that people need to go through the steps described in the grieving cycle and that help is required if they are to progress through it as quickly and painlessly as possible. If assistance is not provided, then it is often found that they "stick" in the part of the cycle (in the areas up to step 5: - bargaining) commonly known as the "pits of despair". It is important that people get past this stage to ensure the success of the programme.

APPENDIX B: PROGRAMME PLANNING.

Introduction

The initial preparation of the Programme Plan is usually carried out during the programme definition process/phase - however, it is revisited and updated on an ongoing basis throughout the programme. The importance of a usable plan cannot be underestimated - it is the key to the effective control of the programme. The plan itself does not ensure a successful programme - it is the monitoring and control of the programme measured against the plan that is the key action. This particular technique is particularly important because if done correctly Programme Planning can be invaluable to the Programme Manager. Unfortunately, very often the purpose of the plan and what it must contain is not clearly understood and as a result it becomes either an irrelevance or a burden to the Programme Manager.

The programme plan process

- **Identify potential new and existing projects**
- **Prepare/obtain estimates**
  Duration, resource requirements, cost and benefits
- **Prepare Project to Programme Contribution Matrix**
- **Prepare Project Mandates for the Projects**
- **Prepare Programme Plan - match required benefits profile**
- **Identify and agree Programme Milestones**
- **Identify and Agree Programme Review points**
- **Identify and confirm dependencies and handshakes**
- **Update Risk Analysis, Benefits Realisation and Sustainability Plan**

The Programme Plan includes more than the Gantt Chart and should comprise several major deliverables. These deliverables are best developed in the order described in this section, although in some situations this order may be modified to reflect prevailing circumstances. What is vital is that they are all developed prior to the programme being commissioned as they contain information critical to the successful implementation, monitoring and control of the programme.

Identify potential new and existing projects

This first step consists of obtaining a list of the new and existing projects that are to be subsumed into the programme, together with the relevant project documents (e.g. Project Mandate or Brief, existing plans). It is important to ensure documents are accurate representations of existing projects and are not out of date.

Prepare/obtain estimates

The Programme Manager needs an up-to-date estimate of the timescales, resources and costs required to complete the projects within the programme. It is important that the Programme Manager clearly identifies what information is needed and collects it at an appropriate level. This means that they do not need not to know all the details about the proposed and existing projects, but summary information in a consistent format across all projects.

In particular the major milestones in each project, resources required, the costs and the elapsed timescales for the project. This process is performed in most organisations as part of the definition and agreement of the Project Mandate or Brief process.

Duration, resource requirement, cost and benefits

The information collected from the previous step is supplemented with information from the business case for each project, so that a clear picture of the resource requirements, costs and potential benefits of the projects can be collated. It is important that these benefits reflect the worth of the project to the programme and not just at the project level, as this can be a serious underestimation of the total or real worth of the project.

To ensure that this information is collected in a structured way use of a Project to Programme Contribution Matrix is recommended (see appendix c).

Prepare project mandates or brief – confirm with projects

Contents of a Project Mandate or Brief include:

- **B ackground and aim of the programme**
- **O bjectives - SMART (S pecfic M easurable, A chievable, R elevant, T ime banded.)**
- **S cope - Physical, Logical, People**
- **A ssumptions (Before and After)**
- **R eporting and management arrangements.**

The Project Mandate and/or Brief is one of the major interfaces between the programme and the constituent projects. The Project Mandate and/or Brief is not only used to commission the project it is also part of the business processes by the organisation. The key element in this process is the initial confirmation of the Mandate and/or Brief with the Project Board and Project Manager. Once the Project Initiation Document has been completed, it is used to ensure that the project is contributing what is expected/required by the programme.

This Project Mandate and/or Brief are used as the basis for the Project Initiation Document and the Programme Definition which are regularly reviewed by both the programme and project management organisation structures respectively to ensure that both the programme and the projects are still within their agreed scope.

Prepare programme plan - match required benefits profile

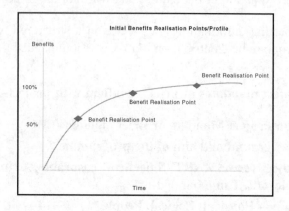

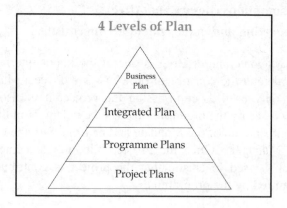

There are four levels of plan within most organisations:-

- the long range business plan;
- the overall integrated plan showing the key milestones and interdependencies across the programmes;
- the plans at programme level;
- the individual project plans.

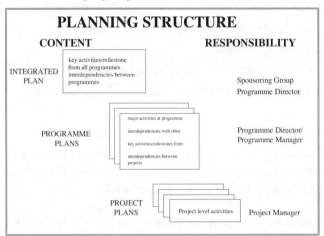

When preparing the Programme Plan, the Programme Manager must sequence the projects in the programme so that they will provide a benefit stream that matches the required Benefits Realisation Profile (see Appendix D).

However, adopting this approach can result in what appears to be an uneconomic or inefficient sequence of executing the projects. This is perfectly acceptable providing that the sequence does not substantially increase the costs of a programme i.e. put it outside of its agreed tolerance. The reasoning behind this approach may be that if the organisation does not achieve the required benefits in the agreed timescales, the whole reason for the programme may nullified.

Programme Managers Companion

The ingenuity required to develop such a plan can be considerable, as can the number of people the Programme Manager will need to discuss the plan with, so that they can be assured it is attainable before submission to the Programme Director for approval.

Identify and agree Programme Milestones

Defining Programme Milestones - Do select those that are:
- **Milestones important to the programme.**
- **Obtaining Benefits.**
- **Commitments for expenditure or resources.**
- **Strategic decisions points outside the programme**

However:
- **Beware of overcomplicating the plan.**
- **Follow the concept that the milestone or review must add value or is a programme decision points (Programme Director or Sponsoring Group level).**

The definition of Programme Milestones can be problematic because there are many candidates for this exalted position. These include;

- points in the programme where large commitments are made - resources, or contracts or methods of approach;
- points where business benefits are realised;
- points where major changes in existing processes, procedures or attitudes occur;
- points in the programme that correspond and interact with business processes operated by the organisation/departments;
- significant points in one or more of the projects.

What is important in selecting which of these to adopt, is to follow the rule of selecting and using those that the Programme Director will recognise and can use in the strategic decision making processes.

As a general guide the least important of these are usually delivery milestones from the projects. However, key delivery milestones for the most important projects within the programme can often be important to the programme as a whole.

Identify and agree programme review points

- **Major Benefits Realisation Points**
- **Commitments for expenditure or resources**
- **Strategic decision points outside the programme**

As with all projects, there is a need for the progress made with the programme to be monitored at specific points to ensure that it is on track and that the reason for the programme and the method of approach being deployed, are still valid.

In defining the Programme Plan the Programme Manager must identify suitable points for this review. When looking for these points, the general rule to follow is to select those review points which coincide with points in the programme where major benefits are to realised, decisions are required, or, where major decisions (made outside the programme) which affect the programme are made.

These points in the programme are also referred to as 'end of Tranche'. At this point in the programme there is time to reflect on what has been achieved and what is left to achieve. These give a chance to reassess the remainder of the programme and to effect control or other action as required. (see appendix e for progress reviews).

Identify and confirm dependencies and "handshakes"

- These are the Vital Control points for the Programme Manager
- Define only those vital to the programme
- Beware of overly complex "wiring diagrams"
- Define and agree the interdependencies and handshakes with other Programme and Project Managers
- Ensure the deliverable join up!

There are two types of such relationships - one is known as interdependencies and the other as "handshaking" products.

"Handshakes" are where there is a direct relationship between the deliverables or work packages, whilst interdependencies are those that have a looser connection - perhaps with many weeks or months float between them.

In most organisations the initial identification of these "handshakes" and interdependencies is done as part of the Programme Mandate and or Brief process and are then refined and included in the Programme Definition and Programme Plan. As with all elements of the Programme Plan and Programme Definition, these will be revisited and updated as the programme progresses.

An effective way to identify and define the "handshakes" and interdependencies between projects within the programme is by calling a meeting of all the Project Managers. Each makes a presentation about their project and its constituent deliverables or work packages. The other Project Managers can then identify any relationship that their project has with other projects. These are documented either on a Gantt Chart or as a table. Calling together all Programme Managers to identify cross programme links can use a similar process.

Programme Managers Companion

Ref	From	Deliverable	To	Handshake/Interdependency Date
1	GE 1	Prototype quest	GE 2	To test remote access – 6 months
2	GE 3	Remote Access	GE 1	Infrastructure ready for full test – 12 months
3	GE 5	Auto Data collection	GE 4	Trial of new system – 1 year 9 months
4	GE 7	Installed Hardware	GE 8	Trial of software – 2 years 7 months
5	GE 9	Software operational	GE 10	Trial of Presentation software

Update risk analysis, benefits realisation and sustainability plans

- **Risk assessment**
- **Blue print or the Programme Vision**
- **Communication Plan**
- **Change Plan**
- **Programme and Project Management Organisation Structures**
- **Benefits Realisation and Sustainability Plan**

Having prepared the schedule for the programme, the Programme Manager can then update or prepare the remainder of the contents of the Programme Plan.

Of particular note is the risk analysis. (Risk management procedures can be found in Appendix G). This will need to take into account the sequencing of the projects in the programme i.e. the compromises that the Programme Manager has had to adopt in order to meet the required Benefits Profile. It will also need to reflect any other substantial changes to the potential risks of the programme.

Finally the Programme Plan is also used to update the Benefits Realisation and Sustainability Plan so that it reflects the arrangements now included in the Programme Plan for the realisation of the planned benefits.

APPENDIX C: PREPARING THE PROJECT–PROGRAMME CONTRIBUTION MATRIX.

The Project- Programme Contribution Matrix includes:

- **all projects (old and new)to be included**
- **work packages, initiatives and Roles and their contribution**
- **contribution which can be measured in terms of**
  Benefits Obtained
  Earned Value Analysis
  Must, Should or could etc.
  Weighting and Ranking Tables
  Difficulty and or Risk
  Etc,

The Project-Programme Contribution Matrix is produced to assist the Programme Manager in developing the Programme Plan. It provides an agreed definition of the relative importance of each of the projects so that they can be included in the programme in the most beneficial sequence.

This matrix helps ensure that there are no functionality or logical gaps in the programme. It is often found that when the matrix is compared to what the programme is designed to achieve, some critical elements are missing. This particularly applies to those relating to the soft or Human Resources issues surrounding the programme.

Example – Programme Contribution Matrix

Project	Benefits (All figures in £K)	% Contribution to Programme
1. Agreed arrangements for transferring budget allocationfrom Local Government Authorities and Government Department (Employment) to United Libraries.	Infrastructure basis of all three streams of benefits. Worth 20% of Grand Total of all benefits (£521,105 K x 20%) per full year plus Infrastructure basis of Government Information Systems Stream. 20% of that benefit (£261,000 K x 20%) per full year	(156,421 K) 30.1%
2. Development and implementation of administrative processes to support cross	Infrastructure basis of Job Club Stream. 20% charging for Job Club Service. of benefits (£249,080 K x 20%) per full year	(49,816 K) 9.56%
3. Management of Change.	Infrastructure basis of all three streams of benefits. Worth 10% of Grand Total of all benefits (£521,105 K x 10%) per full year	(52,110 K) 10%
4. Installation of Standalone PC's and Internet connections in each library.	Infrastructure basis of all three streams of benefits Worth 5% of Grand Total of all benefits (£521,105 K x 5%)per full year	(26,055 K) 5%
5. Retraining of existing staff to support Job Clubs and other users of the technology.	Infrastructure basis of Job Club Stream. 20% of benefits (£249,080 K x 20%) per full year	(49,816 K) 9.56%
6. Transfer of Job Clubs from Local Government Authorities/Department of Employment responsibility to United Libraries.	Realisation of Job Club Benefits 25% of benefits (£249,080 K x 25%) per full year	(62,270 K) 11.95%
7. Development of WAN (Intranet) connections to Government Data Network, Department of Employment and employment agencies.	Infrastructure basis of Government Information Systems Stream 20% of benefits (£261,000 K x 20%) per full year	(52,200 K) 10.01%
8. Upgrading of equipment to utilise WAN.	Infrastructure basis of Government Information Systems Stream. 20% of benefits (£261,000 K x 20%) per full year)	(52,200K) 10.01%
9. Development and implementation of administrative processes to support cross charging for Government Information Systems	Benefits Realisation of Government Information Systems Stream. 5% of benefits (£261,000 K x 5%) per full year	(13,050 K) 2.5%
10. Business process Reengineering of Library functions and locations.	Infrastructure basis of Library Restructuring Stream 20% of benefits (£11,025 K x 20%) per full year	(2,205 K) 0.42%
11. Implementation of revised locations.	Benefits Realisation of part of Library Restructuring Stream. 20% of benefits (£11,025 K x 20%) per full year	(2,205 K) 0.42%
12. Implementation of revised Library business processes. (Book procurement, installation	Benefits Realisation of part of Library Restructuring Stream. 25% of benefits (£11,025 K x 25%) per full year	(2,756 K) 0.53%

APPENDIX D: PREPARING THE BENEFITS REALISATION AND SUSTAINABILITY PLAN.

The Benefits Realisation and Sustainability Plan is used to summarise the processes put into place to operate the benefits management regime – this is fundamental to the use of programme management.

The Benefits Realisation and Sustainability Plan is started initially during the Programme Identification Process/Phase at the start of the programme and is updated as the programme progresses and therefore provides a history of how the benefits have, or will be, obtained and sustained.

Step One: ***The Business Vision***
The business vision identifies in general terms the benefits to be obtained and the areas of the organisation that are involved in obtaining them. This definition of the benefits is added to the plan (in row 1).

Step Two: ***The Investment/Benefits Appraisal***
Once the investment/benefits appraisal has been agreed the benefits section (row 1) of the plan is updated to reflect the current situation.

Step Three: ***The Required Benefits Profile***
This document is produced as a result of the acceptance of the Investment Appraisal/Business Case and provides guidance as to what benefits will be obtained and when. This document is used to update the benefits section (row 1) of the plan and by the inclusion of the initial plan of the actions to be used to realise the benefits (row 2).

Step Four: Implementation Option
Once the organisation has identified which of the Implementation Options
is to be adopted, the Benefits Realisation and Sustainability Plan is
updated to reflect the more specific information about how the
programme will be delivered and how the benefits will be obtained. At
this point it may well be possible to identify some or all of the actions
that will be needed to realise the benefits and to identify which of the
business as usual managers will be involved in implementing the changes.
As a consequence rows, 1 and 2 may need to be updated and the agreed
plan and the responsibility section of the Benefits Realisation and
Sustainability Plan (rows 3 and 4) can be completed.

Step Five: Programme Plan
During the development of the Programme Plan, the specific actions that
will realise the benefits are identified and defined. This will enable the
Business Change Manager and the Programme Manager to update the
Benefits Realisation and Sustainability Plan in respect of the actions
planned and the names of the specific managers who will be involved in
their delivery (rows 3 and 4).

Step Six: Benefits Realisation
As the programme and the associated projects are executed, the Business
Change Manager and the Programme Manager work with those business-
as- usual managers whose areas will be responsible for realising and
sustaining the benefits to develop and implement an action plan to
achieve the benefits. This action plan - when agreed - is either attached
to the Benefits Realisation and Sustainability Plan or included in the plan
(row 8). The Benefits Realisation and Sustainability Plan is updated to
reflect the achievements made and any changes to the plan (rows 3,4,5,6)
and included in the regular and end of Tranche review report to the
Programme Director and Sponsoring Group.

Step Seven: ***Programme Closure***
As part of the project and programme closure process, the Programme Manager must ensure that actions and plans are in place to realise all the benefits and to ensure that these are sustained. These actions and plans must be identified in the Benefits Realisation Plan (rows 7 and 8). The Business Change Manager and the Programme Manager must ensure that the managers who are responsible for realising the benefits, understand and formally accept their role in ensuring that the benefits are not eroded over time. An agreed action plan needs to be agreed with the managers responsible. This plan will cover how they will report that the benefits are being sustained to ensure erosion does not occur.

Example – Benefits Realisation and Sustainability Plan

	Benefits No 1	Benefits No 2	Benefits No 3
1. Description Of The Benefit (*Programme Identification*)	Reduction in Benchmark from £.5 to 1.4	Elimination of Process X	Increase in coverage of services
2. Initial Plan (*Programme Definition*)	Will be mainly achieved in department X	Will be accomplished in departments x.y.z	Will affect sales force and invoicing department
3. Agreed Plan (*Programme Implementation*)	1. Introduction of new system. Reduction in X staff and X in maintenance charges 2. Change in Business Process. Reduction in X staff 3. Integrating new systems and process - Further reduction in maintenance charges and staff		
4. Responsibility (*Programme Implementation*)	1. Joe Upton, Head of Administration 2. Jill Willis, Head of Process Improvement. 3. William Smith, Line Supervisor		
5. Achieved To Date (*Updated Each Major Review*)	1. Initial trial underway - maintenance agreements cancelled 2. New process in action (see staff reallocation memo) 3. Not yet started		
6. Achievements Next Period (*Updated Each Major Review*)	1. Pilot installed (see staff reallocation memo 2 2. Further reductions in staff (see staff reallocation memo 3). 3. Underway – Maintenance Agreements cancelled		
7. Manager Responsible for Sustainability (*Programme Closure*)	1. Joe Upton – Headcount down by 16 (to 106) maintenance budget down 100K (to 1,200K) 2. Jill Willis Headcount down by 12 (to 222) 3. William Smith Headcount down by 10 (to 112) maintenance budget down 10K (to 120K)		
8. Supporting Documents	xxxxx.doc xxxxx.wpc xxxxx.xls		

Programme Managers Companion

91

APPENDIX E: PROGRAMME MONITORING AND CONTROL.

The need to define the monitoring, reporting and control process at programme start up.

In the rush and pressure of starting up a programme the Programme Manager often fails to establish and define the programmes monitoring, reporting and control processes. As a consequence when the first progress reports are due not only do the Programme Management Team have to collect the data they also find themselves having to design these processes.

As a consequence not enough consultation, time or thought goes into the production of the information. It can easily become a logistical nightmare to collect the data and (because the report formats and contents were not agreed) deal with the inevitable changes that occur on a regular basis. This causes not only unnecessary work but also seriously affects the ability of the programme to analyse and identify lessons learnt.

It is vital that the Programme Manager and his team – discuss and agree with the following members of the organisation their requirements for information about the programme – **before it starts** and also the format and content of these reports.

- The Sponsoring Group
- The Programme Director
- The Business Change Managers
- Other related Operational Departments
- Finance Department
- Procurement Department
- HR Departments
- Corporate planning or assurance function.

Programme Managers Companion

92

It is vital that the discussion with these groups of staff identifies both the data and information required by them and also the format that the report will take.

To assist this process it is vital that the Programme Management Team prepare "Strawmen" versions of the possible types of report they could provide. These are used to facilitate a discussion between these groups and the Programme Management Team to not only identify what information and data is needed also why they need that information and what they are going to do with it.

Quite often when subjected to such a discussion the needs become wants and the reasons for the information are often simply to keep up to date with what is required. – Identifying this can save considerable effort and paper!

The format of the progress reports

The format chosen for the progress reports is extremely important. This is because it is vital that the recipient of the report assimilates the information within it without the need for further analysis and interpretation. If this is nor achieved then the message it contains may not be received as was intended or even worse not received at all!.

The choices of the format of these reports is extremely large – what is important is that a range of these possible formats is discussed and the most appropriate one selected.

Examples of such reports are as follows

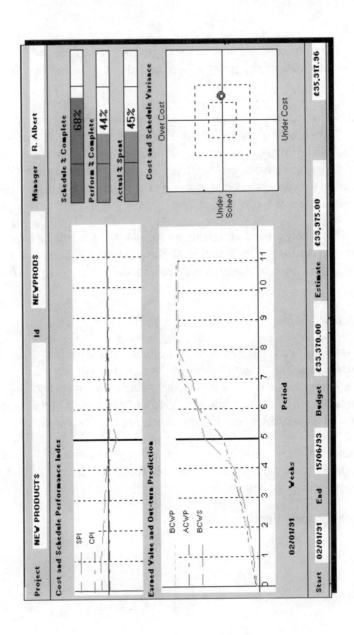

Programme Managers Companion

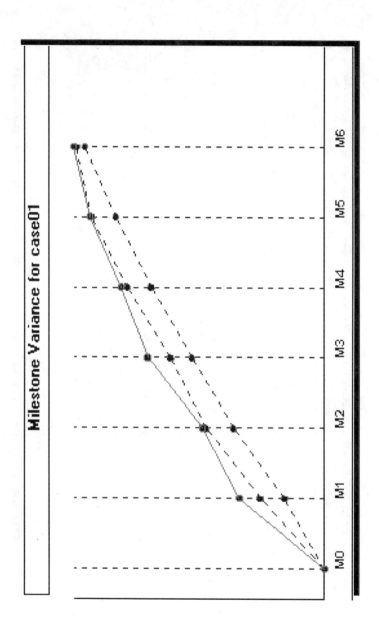

Programme Managers Companion

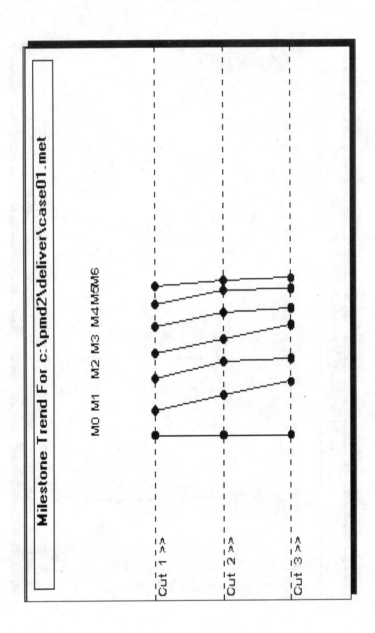

Programme Managers Companion

These report formats are tried and trusted – each achieves passing the information quickly and easily

The purpose of programme monitoring

To measure where we are now - and what is left to do
- **Plan of what we intended to do**
- **Where we are now**
- **Analyses of the impact of progress on the plan**
- **Decide if control action is required**
  More of - Less of - Do something else
- **Prepare new plan**

The key reason for monitoring progress is to identify where a problem exists, or will exist, so that research can be carried out to identify and put into place action to control the problem .

The added value comes not from identifying there is a problem, but from an analysis of the root cause and how the organisation can mitigate it or avoid future problems. Thus the Programme Managers individual focus should be concentrated on the <u>analysis</u> rather than the data collection and collation.

The basis of progress reporting:

In order to monitor progress and identify any problems, it is vital to have defined measurement points. These are the Programme Milestones that are identified and agreed when the Programme Plan is first developed and amended as the plan is updated through the programme.

The Types of Milestones

- Programme Level (significant points in the programme
  Business benefits delivery point, resource or method
  commitments, major handshakes or interdependencies,
  major changes in culture or attitudes
- Project Level (significant points in the project
  Technical development point, work package or products
  delivered, technical or business decisions

There are number of milestones that can be monitored by the Programme
Manager - what is important is that the monitoring process and supporting
information systems have been carefully thought out, agreed and
implemented. This development of the monitoring and control process
should not be carried out by the Programme Manager as they are
preparing the progress reports. This should be avoided, as it is not only
uneconomic, it also diverts the Programme Manager from the most
valuable part of the process - the analysis.

Progress Reviews

The three main types of reviews

- Regular

  Progress expenditure risks and benefits (the programme first
  then the projects)
- End of Tranche (as the regular review plus

  Programme Definition, updated Programme Plan, Benefits
  Realised, and programme approach
- Exception

There are three types of reviews conducted by the Programme Manager on a regular basis through the programme. The first two types of reviews are conducted at defined intervals and to defined formats.

Regular reporting:

- **Monthly to Programme Director**
- **Regular update to the Sponsoring Group**
- **Quarterly to Board***

*This frequency is liable to change for different phases of the programme, as directed by the Sponsoring Group or Board.

Monthly to Programme Director:
All Project Managers normally complete a progress report on a monthly basis and submit them to the Programme Manager. The Programme Manager with the assistance of the Programme Support Office prepares a programme level report. The report must covers five performance variables - progress, risks, expenditure, financial and non-financial benefits. A narrative should accompany these programme submissions and this report will be circulated prior to the Programme Director's meeting. Supporting information will be available in the form of Programme Plans, risk register, issues log, cost reports.

Typical Report

	Costs £	Benefits £	Benefits: Non financial	Progress	Risk	Status
Programme☐ Performance					**Overall Status**	
PROGRAMME						
PROJECTS						
1						
2						
3						
Etc.						

The Programme Manager's meeting with the Programme Director reviews the progress against milestones, interdependencies with other programmes, key risks and addresses any major issues that have been raised.

The important part of these types of review is the analysis of the situation that the Programme Manager performs. This analysis must be designed to provide the Programme Director and the Sponsoring Group with the information necessary for them to carry out their role of providing the strategic direction and guidance. It is important not to take tactical issues to the Sponsoring Group and thus corrupt the strength of the organisation structure. This corruption results in "responsibility rollover" which manifests itself in the senior management becoming preoccupied with the tactical issues rather than the strategic.

Ongoing performance reviews:

Each programme will report to the Sponsoring Group and the Board on a regular basis as required.

The Programme Director will be responsible for leading on this performance review.

The purpose of the on-going performance review is to ensure that the programmes remain aligned to the strategy and that integration is managed effectively.

The programme level report along with the current version of the Programme Definition is circulated to the Sponsoring Group for pre-reading prior to the meeting.

Quarterly to Board:

On a quarterly basis, the business planning team and the Programme Director and Programme Manager assisted by the Programme Support Office will prepare a written and oral report to the Board which provides a high level consolidated picture of progress across the programme.

The focus of this report will be the progress made in delivering the 'Vision' milestones and identify where any strategic direction or guidance is required. This report will be supported with a Blueprint level report and an updated copy of the Programme Plan, which identifies the remaining key milestones across the agreed time horizons.

Annual strategic review

On an annual basis the Board will review and update the priorities for, and the contents of, the strategic goals and targets, of the organisation and update (if necessary) the contents of the programmes to ensure they support the achievement of the strategic goals and targets.

End of Tranche or programme phase review:

Of these two types of regular reviews the most important is the end of Tranche or programme phase review.

End of Tranche Review Process

- **Preparation - decide and agree When reviews will be held - content and from and with whom**
- **Ensure you have the up-to-date and truthful Programme Plan Progress reports, Exception Reports**
- **Check the Validity of your analysis and action plan**

This end of Tranche review is particularly important because, in addition to the review of how much progress has been made in executing the programme, it also reviews the benefits or changes obtained by the programme.

In addition the environment in which the programme was commissioned is reviewed and therefore by implication, the business goals and targets that the programme is designed to achieve (see Appendix B).

APPENDIX F: EXCEPTION PROCESS

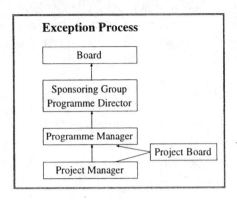

The Programme Manager regularly monitors the programme to identify if the programme is still within the agreed programme definition, especially when a major issue or risk is identified. In these cases, if the Programme Manager identifies that the programme either has, or will exceed the agreed plan and the allocated tolerance, this must be drawn to the attention of the Programme Director and if extremely serious, the Sponsoring Group as soon as possible. The Programme Manager must prepare a paper which describes what has happened - an analysis of why it has happened, the impact on the programme and the plan for either recovering from the problem, and/or the cost that the programme will incur.

This report and the associated plans are then discussed with the Programme Director and the Sponsoring Group and the relevant decision made. All the actions carried out by the Programme Manager must be noted in the programme exception log (or the programme log or diary), as must the decisions made about the situation and the resulting changes made to the programme definition and the Programme Plan.

If the issue cannot be resolved at programme level, the Programme Director can raise it as an emergency issue to the Sponsoring Group or Board during the allotted agenda time reserved for programme performance review.

Programme Directors are required to

- Inform the Sponsoring Group or Board in advance of the meeting, including the time required;
- Provide the Sponsoring Group or Board with a statement of the purpose, process and desired output for the issue.

APPENDIX G: RISK MANAGEMENT.

There are four levels of risk in most organisations in the programme/project environment.

Project risks:

Risks identified at project level, which are related solely to the individual project, are wholly owned and managed by the Project Manager. If a risk affects areas outside of the Project Managers' areas of responsibility and could have a major impact on the programme, the risk should be referred to the Programme Manager for consideration as a programme risk.

Programme risks:

The Programme Manager reviews the risks escalated by projects and if deemed appropriate as a programme risk, it should be assessed at programme level using the group risk profiling method. The Programme Manager and team also identify any programme wide risks that have not been escalated up from projects. E.g. risks impacting the benefits of the programme as well as the sustainability, risks around interfaces between projects within the programme and risks around interfaces to other programmes.

Programme risks should be regularly reviewed and monitored by the Programme Director.

Blueprint risks:

All *newly identified* programme risks must be forwarded to the relevant Programme Managers of other programmes (sometimes this is done by the Programme Support Office) for impact assessment on other programmes. If it is uncertain as to which programme is affected they may be forwarded, as relevant, to the Sponsoring Group or Board to decide which programme/s should take ownership of that risk.

Any programme risks which, as a result of regular monitoring, *change significantly* and are considered to have become a risk to other programmes should also be forwarded as previously described.

Business risks:

Those risks considered as business risks need to be considered in respect of their impact on the whole business as opposed to the impact on an individual programme. Therefore programme business risks are combined with those normal business risks identified by business units and presented to the Board for assessment and action.

Risk action:

All programme and project risks are allocated to a risk owner and an action plan is identified to manage each risk.

These action plans will be reviewed and updated by the Programme Director and Programme Manager and if required the Sponsoring Group. The relevant risk owner will feed back the updated action plans to the Programme Manager (this process may be overseen by the Programme Support Office) and the information will be provided to the relevant Programme Managers (for onward transmission to Project Managers if applicable).

Risk management structure and process:

There is a fundamental policy requirement within most organisations for employees to manage risk within their own area of responsibility. This basic policy is quite often delivered within a framework based around "risk profiling". This is necessary to ensure a consistent approach to the identification, management and reporting of risk.

Typical **Risk Framework.**

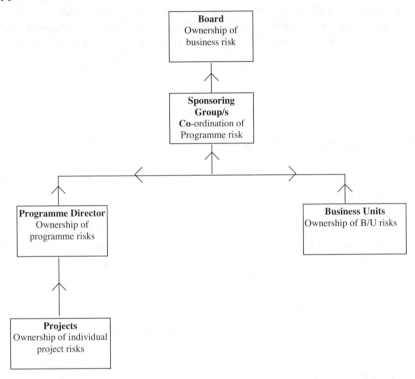

Project/Programme/Business Risk:

There are various text book definitions of risk, however, confusion does arise in understanding the difference between project risk, programme risk and business risk. The answer is basically one of scope:

Project risks are those that threaten the delivery of a specific project and are limited to the lifecycle of the project. They should be profiled and scored in relation to that project.

Programme risks are wider in scope. Some project risks will also be relevant at the programme level. Equally there will be other business or environmental factors that may put a programme at risk. All risks relating to the delivery of the programme benefits should be included.

Business unit risks are like programme risks, but threaten achievement of that particular business unit's objectives, or its operations.

Business risks at the highest level on the overall business risk profile are so significant that they threaten achievement of the key business objectives or strategies. Due to the important nature of these risks they are managed at Board and Business Unit Leader level.

Note: However, in some cases an important project risk may actually be relevant at all levels e.g. a key automation project. However the general rule is that risk scores are not portable - risks escalated from one level to the next should be assessed in that wider environment.

A final point on this is that the key parts of risk management are identifying risks, and actually **doing something about them** - assessment is just a means of ranking risk relatively and does not provide solutions.

Projects/Programmes:

A key principle in developing the approach is that all areas of the business should adopt the same approach and, use the same tools and techniques as far as possible.

The following summarises the typical processes used within the project/programme arena: -

- each project will identify and manage risks to the delivery of that project against the criteria of cost, time, and quality/performance;

- each project will maintain a risk log/project risk register laid out in the organisations standard format, and will report significant new or escalating risks to the Programme Manager using the reporting format;

- each Programme Director will maintain a risk profile in the standard format (assessed using the organisations standard format);

- the Programme Director, Programme Manager assisted by the Programme Support Office will co-ordinate the process, and report monthly to the Sponsoring Group any significant new or escalating risks.

- additionally, the Programme Manager and the Programme Support Office will report to the Sponsoring Group or Board any risks which have been identified that are relevant for another programme or business unit to be aware of or actively manage.

Business units:

Business unit risks are currently reported via the business planning process, and additionally, key business risks are usually updated quarterly for the Board. Each business unit must identify any major new or escalating risks requiring attention at Board.

Summary:

Risk management is already well embedded in everyday activity within organisations. By sharing information and ensuring that important risks are escalated to the right level the organisation can make even better use of the risk information they have, without creating an industry.

Example Risk Assessment Method

Generic or Corporate Risk – A Risk identified as applying to all programmes

Specific Risk – An identified risk to this programme (may be part of a Generic or Corporate Risk)

Impact - list the effects that the occurrence of the risk would have. Remember there may be indirect or consequential impacts in addition to those first considered when the risk was identified.

Controls/Monitoring - list the countermeasures/controls/monitoring mechanisms **currently** in place that reduce the likelihood of the risk occurring or mitigate its impact.

Likelihood/Impact Scores - risks should be scored **after** taking into account the controls/monitoring considered above, using the standard definitions as below:

Total Risk Score - add the impact scores together and multiply by the likelihood score to produce the total risk score.

Risk Owner - this is usually the senior manager ultimately responsible for the risk - (often the manager with the respective reserved power in the case of business risk).

Action Planning - identify what further actions might be taken to manage the risk

Business and programme risk scoring method:

Likelihood		Score
Highly Probable	– the event will almost certainly occur	6
Probable	– the event is likely to occur	5
Possible	– the event could occur	4
Improbable	– the event probably won't occur	3
Unlikely	– there is little chance of the event occurring	2
Highly Unlikely	– almost no chance of the event occurring	1

Impact		
High	– serious effect, probably widespread	3
Medium	– damaging effect, probably localised	2
Low	– little or no effect	1

for each of the following criteria

External	– including customers, clients and impact on society
Financial	– results including income and expenditure
People	– including leadership, staff and agents
Continuity	– of operations or delivery of programme benefits

Project risk scoring method:

Probability and impact Scales

The probability of occurrence and severity of potential impacts of each identified risk can be assessed using agreed scales. Example scales are given below.

Probability

	Scale	Probability
Very Low	1	< 10%
Low	2	10-30%
Medium	3	30-50%
High	4	50-70%
Very High	5	> 70%

Impact

To ensure consistency of assessment, the meaning of each scale point should be individually defined for relevance to the particular project.

	Scale	Impact on Example Project		
		Timescales (Months)	Cost (% Increase)	Performance
Very Low	1	< 1	< 5%	Failure to meet a minor acceptance criterion.
Low	2	1-2	5-10%	Failure to meet more than one minor acceptance criterion.
Medium	3	3-4	10-15%	Shortfall in meeting acceptance criteria.
High	4	4-6	15-30%	Significant shortfall in meeting acceptance criteria.
Very High	5	>6	> 30%	Failure to meet acceptance criteria.

Risk Register or Log

GENERIC RISK	SPECIFIC	IMPACT RISK	Controls/ Monitoring mechanisms	Likelihood	Impact	Total Risk Score	Risk Owner	Action Plan

Programme Managers Companion

113

Appendix H: Issues Process.

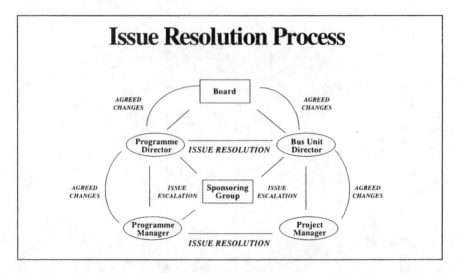

Issue Resolution Process

A programme issue can be any event, situation, concern which may impact on the programme in either a beneficial or harmful way. An issue may be raised by any member of the programme organisation structure

Step One: *Resolution at local level*

The Programme Manager discusses the issue with the relevant Project Manager/s to identify if the issue can be resolved by them within the tolerance allowed by the Programme Director or Project Board and also whether it is purely a project or a programme matter.

If the analysis shows that resolving the issue does not materially change either the programme or the project scope they can then instigate any action that is needed. Any changes that effect the programme must be notified to the programme director in the normal reporting process.

Programme Managers Companion

Step Two   *Escalation 1- Programme Director*

If the analysis shows that the issue cannot be resolved at local level then the escalation process is operated. At programme level the issue is referred to the Programme Director who decides if the issue can be resolved at their level.

Optional Additional Step

If the issue affect more than one programme the Programme Director and Programme Manager must discuss the issue with the other programme/s and decide which Sponsoring Group should deal with the Issue.

Step Three   *Escalation 2-Sponsoring Group*

The Programme Director raises the issue with the Sponsoring Group. The discussion must include an explanation of the issue, the impact of the issue, the proposed or available courses of action, a recommended course of action and a proposed implementation plan.

The decision from these discussions must also be formally recorded.

Step Four   *Escalation 3 - Board*

If the issue has not been resolved by the Sponsoring Group involved then the Programme Director must take it to the Board for a final decision. The discussion must be supported with a paper explaining the issue, the impact of the issue, the proposed or available courses of action - a recommended course of action and a proposed implementation plan.

All the above process is documented in the Programme Issue Log, maintained by the Programme Manager.

Appendix I: Benefits Profile

Introduction

One of the key reasons for the use of Programme Management approach is to ensure that the programme provides the required benefits.

This section describes the how the Benefits (Realisation) Profile is constructed and how its is used throughout the life of the programme.

Where the Benefits profile starts

When the Sponsoring Group decide that a programme is needed it must also define the key benefits that the programme is to provide and when these are required if the organisation is to achieve its business plan.

This information is handed to the Programme Director at the start of the programme as part of the Programme Mandate. Without this information the Programme Director and the Programme Manager have no real start point for the Programme Brief and the Programme Definition processes.

The information provided by the Sponsoring Group may be high level as the following examples show.

Required Benefits Timetable Programme 1

Benefit	When required
Automatic generation of questionnaires - 20%	Year One
Conversion to most interviews by Email or telephone - 50%	Year Two
Full operation of Golden Eye - 100%	Year Three

Required Benefits Timetable Programme 2

Benefit	When required
Knowledge of critical areas of infrastructure - 20%	3 months
Proposals for implementing Just In Time Engineering - 40%	5 months
Introduction of Just in Time on new workload - 60%	9 months
Introduction of Just in Time Engineering on remaining workload - 100%	12 months

Constructing the Method of Approach and Programme Implementation Options

As part of the Programme Definition process the Programme Manager will need to identify the various options that could be used to implement the programme and ultimately to select the one upon which the Programme Plan is to be based.

This is achieved by first translating the required benefits information provided by the Sponsoring Group into a simple cumulative benefits and time graph which shows how - in a graphical form when the required benefits are to be achieved.

To enable this graph to be constructed the Programme Manager must translate the information provided by the Sponsoring Group into an assessment of the their contribution to the whole outcome of the programme as a percentage.

In some programmes this a is relatively straightforward- - if however this cannot be easily effected what matters is that the methodology used (not which one is used) and the assessed contribution is agreed.

The resulting graph can look like the following example.

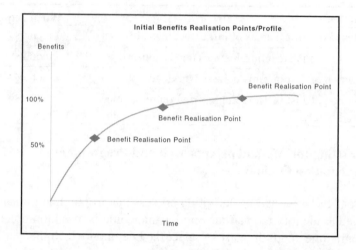

Once this graph is completed the Programme Manager together with experienced Project Managers and other specialists then identify the various implementation options that could be used to deliver the programme. The classic routes are often referred to as the *"Quick and Dirty, Build it Slow Build it Right and Something in between" options.*

These three options are then assessed as to how they match the required profile and also the risks and any other issues associated with them are identified The Programme Manager will discuss these options and their ability to deliver the required benefits and their risks and issues with the Programme Director. The resultant decision as to which option to adopt may well need to be ratified by the Sponsoring Group.

The agreed option and its associated Benefits Profile are then used as the basis of the Programme Plan and the Benefits Realisation Plan.

The following is an example of three options shown as compared to the original Benefits Profile.

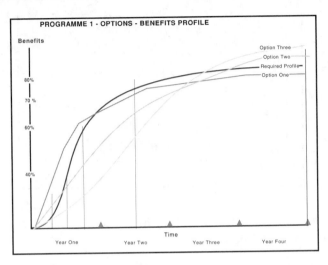

Developing the Programme Plan

Having agreed which of the implementation options is to be used and the resulting Benefits Profiles the Programme Manager, together with the Project Manager's then construct the Programme Plan.

This process consists of identifying what projects are needed to ensure the required Benefits Profile is delivered and then scheduling these projects to meet that the plan. A graphical representation of the Programme Plan showing the projects and the required Benefits Profile is usually developed to confirm that all the required components are present before the programme is commissioned.

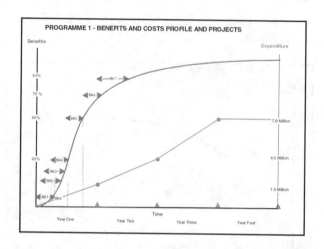

PROGRAMME 1 - BENEFITS AND COSTS PROFILE AND PROJECTS

Identifying the handshakes and interdependencies required to achieve the required benefits

Having defined the outline of the Programme Plan the Programme Manager and the Project Managers then identify the deliverables within the projects that will link or match or handshake together to deliver the befits. The Business Change Managers also provide a major input to this process, as they will define the activities that will realise the benefits.

This list of interdependencies and handshakes can be shown on the Programme Plan and or as a table.

Programme Managers Companion

120

The following diagram and table illustrates these handshakes

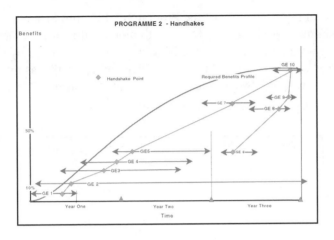

Ref	From	Deliverable	To	Handshake/Interdependency Date
1	BK 1	Draft Report	BK 3	Needed to inform plan 3 months
2	BK 2	Draft Report	BK 4	Need to inform plan 6 months
3	BK 3	Draft report	BK 4	Need to build product 6 months
4	BK4,BK2	Final report	BK 5	Basis of this report 9 months
5	BK 5	Contract	BK 6	Kick off 15 months
6	BK 6	Contract	BK7	Final arrangements 18 months
T1	BK D1	Sign off	BKD 4	Application Platform stable ASAP
T 2	BK D4	Docman system running	BK D6	Bill payment process reengineering 16 months
T3	BK D6	Payment system	BK D7, BK D8	Customer errors programme starts 18 months

The handshakes information is then used as the basis of the Benefits Realisation Plan - this describes all the key activities that will used to deliver the required benefits.

Monitoring the progress made.

The graphical representation of the Programme Plan produced as part of the Programme Definition are also used to monitor the progress achieved by the programme in delivering the benefits. This is achieved by plotting the achieved benefits on the Programme Plan and using this as the basis of discussion with the Programme Director and Sponsoring Groups in respect of any control action that is needed.

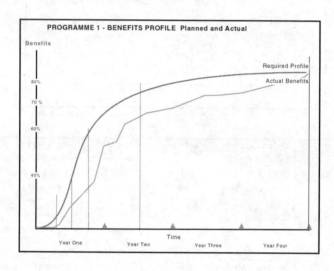